Buying, Owning, & Selling a Condominium

Buying, Owning, & Selling a Condominium

Douglas A. Gray

McGraw-Hill Ryerson
Toronto   Montreal

Buying, Owning, & Selling a Condominium
A Guide for Canadians

First published in 1989 by
McGraw-Hill Ryerson Limited
330 Progress Avenue
Scarborough, Ontario M1P 2Z5

Canadian Cataloguing in Publication Data
Gray, Douglas A.
  Buying, owning, and selling a condominium

Includes index.
ISBN 0-07-549681-X

1. Condominiums—Canada   I. Title.

HD7287.67.C3G73 1988   643'.2   C89-093184-4

This publication is designed to provide accurate and authoritative information on the subject matter covered. However, laws are constantly changing, and the examples given are intended to be general guidelines only.

This book is sold with the understanding that neither the author nor the publisher is engaged in rendering legal, accounting, or other professional advice. If such advice or other assistance is required, the personal services of a competent professional should also be sought.

Printed and bound in Canada
1 2 3 4 5 6 7 8 9 10 W 8 7 6 5 4 3 2 1 0 9

OTHER BOOKS BY DOUGLAS A. GRAY

Start and Run a Profitable Consulting Business
The Entrepreneur's Complete Self-Assessment Guide
Marketing Your Product (co-authored with Donald Cyr)
The Complete Canadian Small Business Guide
(co-authored with Diana Gray)

CONTENTS

Charts

Appendixes

PREFACE

Buying or selling a condominium can be a confusing process. Many people do not even know what a condominium is, or the legal structure and responsibilities that are involved in owning one. A book was therefore needed that explained, step by step, what a buyer, seller, or owner of a condominium needs to consider in order to make informed and prudent choices. This guide is designed to fulfill that need.

Many people have heard of residential or resort co-operatives (profit or non-profit) and timeshares, but do not fully understand the nature and implications of these types of shared living space. Often, decisions on timeshares are made under time pressure, with regrettable results. With this in mind, I have provided an explanation of the various types of timeshares and co-operatives. (Many timeshares also involve condominium ownership.)

The legal, financial, and practical issues involved in buying, owning, and selling a condominium are described in detail. In addition, there are samples, checklists, charts, and tables that you can refer to as you go along if you wish. You will also find the appendixes to be beneficial: there is a glossary to help you comprehend the jargon, a suggested readings section that lists Canadian and American books that might interest you, and a section that lists sources of further information. This last appendix provides names, contact addresses, and phone numbers.

The content of this book is based on (1) my own experience as a real estate and commercial lawyer, (2) research of the literature, and (3) vicarious experience through extensive interviews with others in the condominium industry—lawyers, realtors, developers, management companies, insurance and mortgage brokers, bankers and condominium owners, investors, and renters.

I hope you enjoy this book, and find the information helpful and encouraging. If you would like to provide some feedback or obtain a brochure of further educational material, please refer to the last page.

D.A.G.

ACKNOWLEDGEMENTS

I am grateful for the kind assistance given me by many parties, including the Canada Mortgage and Housing Corporation, the Canadian Real Estate Association, the Canadian Bankers' Association, and Hamilton Mortgage Group Ltd.

Many thanks also to Royal LePage and the Co-operative Housing Foundation of Canada for their generous permission to use material from their publications.

I would like to express my appreciation to my copy editor, Rodney Rawlings, and my general editors, Denise Schon and Glen Ellis, for their patience, encouragement, and insightful suggestions.

Last but not least, I would like to dedicate this book to my wife and partner Diana, whose unfailing support and assistance makes all things possible.

CHAPTER

1

Understanding Condominiums

INTRODUCTION

Condominiums are a popular form of shared home ownership in Canada representing approximately 400,000 homes, with Ontario, British Columbia, and Alberta (in that order) having the most condominium owners. Almost 20 to 25% of all Canadian residential sales in many major cities are for condominium apartments or townhouses. Condominiums represent a relatively recent form of shared ownership in Canada, the first one having been constructed just over 20 years ago.

The word *condominium* refers to a specific form of shared legal ownership. Although this book concentrates primarily on residential condominiums, there are other types, including resort and commercial.

This book will cover the important aspects of condominium ownership that you should know about if you are considering buying, owning, or selling a condominium. It will include the legal, financial, and practical considerations, and the many options available to you. The book also covers other forms of shared ownership such as co-operatives and co-ownership. Timesharing is also discussed. By the time you have completed the book, you should have a clear idea of whether the condominium concept is for you, and if so, how to choose wisely and avoid the pitfalls.

Several areas will be covered in this first chapter, including an overview of the condominium structure and community living, the advantages and disadvantages of condominiums, types of condominiums, condominium operation and management, rights and responsibilities of condominium ownership, and dealing with disputes. Also included are sections on selecting the right condominium for your needs, selling a condominium, and investing in a condominium.

A. THE CONDOMINIUM CONCEPT

1. What Is a Condominium?

Condominium does not imply a specific structural form, but a legal form. Condominiums (called co-proprietorships in Quebec) may be detached, semi-detached, row-houses, stack townhouses, duplexes, or apartments. They can even be building lots, subdivisions, or mobile home parks. Whatever the style, a residential unit is specified and is owned outright by the individual owner in fee simple. The rest of the property including land, which is called the *common elements* in most provinces, is owned in common with the other owners. For example, an owner would own a fractional share of the common elements in the development. If there are 50 condominium owners, then each individual owner would own 1/50 as tenants in common of the common elements. The legislation of each province can vary, but it is always designed to provide the legal and structural framework for the efficient management and administration of each condominium project. Once the project documents are registered, the project is brought into legal being as a form of tenure.

The part of the condominium which you will own outright is referred to as the *unit* in most provinces. You will have full and clear title to this unit when you purchase it, which will be legally registered in your name in the land registry office in your province. The precise description of the common elements, and exactly what you own as part of your unit, may differ from development to development, but in any event it will be provided for in the documents prepared and registered for each condominium.

Common elements generally include walkways, driveways, lawns and gardens, lobbies, elevators, parking areas, recreational facilities, storage areas, laundry rooms, stairways, plumbing, electrical systems and portions of walls, ceilings and floors, and other items. Parts of the common elements may be designated for the exclusive use of one or more of the individual unit owners, in which case these are called *limited common elements*. In other words, they are limited for the use only of specific owners. Examples would include parking spaces, roof gardens, balconies, storage lockers, and front and back yards.

Condominiums can be built on freehold or leasehold properties. These descriptions are covered in the next chapter. A condominium can also be in a stratified format, where a legal description for the unit is allocated in a vertical dimension. In other words, if you live in a condominium apartment on the 30th floor, there is a precise legal description in the land registry office for that specific unit in the complex. Another form is a bare land condominium. In this example, it would be similar to a building lot subdivision with individual units owned by the unit holders, although the units would appear as detached homes. The rest of the land would be considered common elements.

A condominium development is administered by various legal structures set out in provincial legislation. This is covered in detail later in this chapter.

2. The Concept of Community Living

The concept of community living is very old. In fact, studies show that the legal arrangement for property ownership similar to today's condominium concept dates back to 2,500 years ago in the Middle East. The concept was revived in Europe approximately 200 years ago, and spread to Brazil 50 years ago when that country passed its own condominium ownership legislation. Other countries have followed within the last 30 years, including Puerto Rico, Cuba, and New South Wales in Australia.

The United States adopted the condominium idea in 1961 and now almost every state has pertinent legislation. In Canada the first province to introduce condominium legislation was Alberta in 1966, followed by British Columbia the following month. Ontario passed legislation in 1967, and since then other provinces have followed suit with similar legislation under various names. In 1967 the federal government, under the National Housing Act, provided mortgage funds for the first time for condominium construction through the Canada Mortgage and Housing Corporation.

There are many reasons why the condominium concept has been economically very attractive for purchasers: better land utilization, price competitiveness, built-in amenities, and convenient locations and designs. There is also a wide price range, from $50,000 to over a million dollars depending on the features, level of luxury, and location.

Large segments of the market find the multi-family residential development concept an attractive alternative for their lifestyles, due to the low maintenance required and the opportunity for equity appreciation. Condominium ownership appeals to active young singles, couples without children, couples with children, and pre-retirement and retired couples or singles. Many developments are geared specifically to these segments or to a mixture of these segments.

Two other forms of shared ownership are sometimes confused with condominium ownership: co-operatives and co-ownership. Although there are many similarities in terms of the administration and operation of these developments, there are considerable legal and financial differences. These are discussed in more detail in Chapters 4 and 5, but in summary: (1) A co-operative is a legal structure in which individuals purchase shares in the co-operative corporation in the same way that a person would buy shares in any company. Therefore the individual owns a portion of a company or non-profit society which in turn owns the land and the buildings on it. There is no individual ownership of land in a co-operative arrangement. (2) In a co-ownership arrangement, a number of individuals have part-ownership in a building or a condominium. For example, in the case of a timeshare condominium, 52 people could own one week each, which would represent 1/52 tenancy in common legal interest in the property; each owner would also own an equivalent percentage of that condominium unit's percentage in the overall common elements.

The concept of condominium living is not right for everyone, as it involves not only individual ownership in the unit and shared ownership in other property, but also adherence to rules and regulations, and shared rulership.

3. Advantages and Disadvantages of Condominium Ownership

In any situation of shared ownership and community living there are advantages and disadvantages. An overview of these follows:

(a) Advantages
- Protection from arbitrary rent increases
- Ready availability of financing as a single-family house
- Range of prices, locations, types of structures, sizes, and architectural features available
- Availability of amenities such as swimming pool, tennis courts, health clubs, community centre, saunas, hot tubs, exercise rooms, sun decks, etc.
- Benefits of home ownership in terms of participation in the real estate market and potential growth in equity
- Individual ownership of living units with security of tenure and permanence of occupancy
- Pride in home ownership
- Enablement of people of moderate and middle income to own their own home
- Freedom to decorate interior of unit to suit personal tastes
- Enhancement of security by permanence of neighbours and, in many cases, controlled entrances
- Elimination of many of the problems of upkeep and maintenance often associated with home ownership, since maintenance is usually the responsibility of a professional agency or manager
- The fact that it is often considerably cheaper than buying a single-family home because of more efficient use of land and economy of scale
- Investment opportunity for profit if selected carefully

- Good transitional type of home between rental apartments and single-family houses for growing families or singles or couples; conversely, good transition for "empty nesters" who wish to give up their larger family house
- More marketable than a profit co-operative, a non-profit co-operative, or a 99-year lease unit
- Reduction of costs due to responsibilities for repair and maintenance being shared in many cases, as some owners will contribute considerable volunteer work
- Enhancement of social activities and sense of neighbourhood community by relative permanence of residents
- Elected council that is responsible for many business and management decisions
- Participation of owners in the operation of the development, which involves playing a role in budget-setting and approval, decision-making, determination of rules and by-laws, and other matters affecting the democratic operation of the condominium community

(b) Disadvantages

- Real estate appreciation is generally not as high as for a single-family house.
- May be difficult to accurately assess the quality of construction of the project.
- Unacceptable loss of freedom may be experienced through restrictions contained in the rules and by-laws (for example, restriction on the right to rent, restriction on pets, etc.).
- People live closer together, thereby potentially creating problems from time to time; frequent problem areas include the "five *p*'s": *p*ets, *p*arking, *p*ersonality, *p*arties, and *p*eople.
- Flexibility may be affected if circumstances require that the condominium be sold in a limited time, as condominiums generally sell slower than single-family houses.
- Money is tied up in the condominium ownership, which may affect immediate liquidity needs in certain circumstances.
- One could be paying for maintenance and operation of amenities that one has no desire or intention to use.
- Management of the condominium council is by volunteers, who may or may not have the appropriate abilities and skills.
- There is possible apathy of owners, so that it is always the same people who are able and willing to serve on council.
- Some elected councils behave in an autocratic fashion.
- Mix between living in a single-family house and in a landlord-tenant relationship could cause conflict and frustration depending on people's needs, expectations, and past housing experience.

B. TYPES OF CONDOMINIUMS

There are numerous types of condominium formats for residential, rec-reational, resort, and commercial purposes. Here is an overview of the most common options.

1. Residential Condominiums

Residential condominiums can be found in either the metropolitan or the suburban setting. In the metropolitan setting the most common formats are:

- A modern high-rise apartment building
- A three-to-five-storey new mid-rise building
- A converted older building that formerly consisted of rental apartments
- A building where the street-level floor is owned jointly by the con-dominium corporation members (the unit owners) and which is rented out to retailers to help offset the common maintenance fees of the residential condominiums in the rest of the building
- Same format as the previous, except that the retail space is sold as condominiums

Suburban condominiums tend to be of a different format and are most often found in the form of:

- Cluster housing consisting of multi-unit structures, using housing of two to four units apiece, each with its own private entranceway
- Townhouse-type single-family homes distributed in rows
- Garden apartments consisting of a group of apartment buildings sur-rounding a common green, frequently with each of the floors held by separate condominium owners
- A series of detached single-family homes in a subdivision format, all utilizing the same land and parking areas
- Duplexes, triplexes, or fourplexes

The suburban condominium format tends to make maximum use of the land while creating attractive views, private driveways, and common recreational facilities such as swimming pools, tennis courts, saunas, playground, etc.

Many residential condominium developments, with the conveniences and amenities being offered, have created a complete lifestyle experience. The purpose of these separate developments—restaurants, shopping centres, recreational and entertainment facilities, and care facilities for older people—is to make the condominium community a very distinct and self-contained environment for many people.

2. Recreational/Resort Condominiums

Recreational condominiums can take various forms, including mobile home parks where the "pad" with utility hookups is owned in fee simple with a share in the common property of the rest of the park. Alternatively, it could be in a leasehold format. Another option is to create bare land condominiums in rural, wilderness, or waterfront areas. In these examples an owner could build a cabin with fee simple ownership to the land underneath and own a partial interest in the common elements. The common elements could include a marina, beach, farm, or forest. Common recreational facilities could include a playground or community centre, and assets could include boats or farm animals.

The development in resort areas is extensive and condominiums are frequently built on lakeshores, sea coasts, or island resorts, or in ski country. There are two main types of resort condominiums: those developed for warmer climates and those developed for winter climates.

The warmer-climate type is generally built around a common recreational facility that can be enjoyed throughout the year by the owners, one that includes such facilities as a seashore, lake, marina, or golf course. The buildings tend to range from high-rise apartments to cluster housing.

Winter resort areas tend to be built near popular ski resort developments. Many tend to provide recreational facilities for the summer season as well, such as golf courses, tennis courts, and swimming pools, so that it is a year-round resort. The buildings tend to be in the form of cluster housing, modular housing, or attached townhouses.

People who purchase a recreational or resort condominium tend to:

- Own it outright and use it throughout the year
- Own it outright and rent it when not in use by using the condominium corporation or management company as an agent, using a real estate agent, or renting it independently
- Own a portion of the condominium as a timeshare and use it for one week or more a year; normally each one-week block purchased is equivalent to approximately 1/50 ownership in the condominium

3. Commercial/Industrial Condominiums

Ownership of a commercial or an industrial condominium is similar in concept to the ownership of a residential one. There are various reasons why condominiums for commercial purposes are an attractive alternative to renting space, buying land with a building on it, or buying land and building on it. Some of the benefits include:

- Tax advantages for an owner-occupier of his own business premises including depreciation, expense deductions for mortgage interest, etc.

- Placing a limit on monthly costs by carefully regulating costs through the condominium corporation policies
- Avoiding rent increases
- Shared contribution of costs for features such as maintenance, security, common facilities, and advertising
- Appreciation in value of the condominium over time
- Right to participate in the decision-making relating to the condominium development
- Opportunity to be assured of remaining in a unique location that is commercially attractive
- Removal of the financial risk of owning a complete building
- Provides an alternative if there is a lack of financial capability or desire to own the whole building

The three main types of commercial-use condominiums are: office buildings, professional buildings, and industrial parks.

(a) Office Buildings

The concept of condominium office buildings is not new. For example, Brazil was the first Western country to pass condominium ownership legislation in 1928 and most office buildings in that country are now owned in that manner. In Canada it is a popular concept in many major cities and involves a cross-section of retail and service businesses operating through the condominium structure.

(b) Professional Buildings

A familiar form of office use is the dental or medical condominium, where each dentist or doctor owns a suite. The nature of a dental or medical office is often such that it does not expand in size as other businesses do. Another advantage for the professional is the possibility of sharing reception areas, central telephone answering, accounting areas, and expensive equipment. It is fairly common in this type of building to sell or lease the street-level condominiums to retail outlets such as pharmacies, laboratory or x-ray service groups, magazine stands, restaurants, etc. Lawyers also own offices in condominium buildings and take the same approach as dentists and doctors in terms of shared office space, reception area, library area, word processing, etc.

(c) Industrial Parks

Industrial parks established on a bare land condominium format are a popular development. They can be advantageous due to the fact that the business can have the individual unit for its industrial or manufacturing needs but can share in the common elements such as docks, loading areas, rail sidings, etc.

C. OPERATION OF THE CONDOMINIUM DEVELOPMENT

The Condominium Act of each province (under various names) is the basic legislative document which sets out the procedural requirements for operation of condominiums. This is supplemented by other legal documents that are specialized for each development such as the project document, by-laws, and rules and regulations. A description of these documents is given in Chapter 2. It is important that you obtain copies of these documents and others, as well as of the Condominium Act, before you finalize your purchase of the condominium. In most cases, people don't review this material thoroughly and understand it before purchasing. By the time you are through this book you will probably appreciate the necessity to be aware of the contents of the laws that will regulate you. A copy of the Act for your province can be obtained from your provincial government. Refer to Appendix A, "Sources of Further Information," for a listing of the appropriate government departments to contact.

The main governing structures are the condominium corporation (referred to as the *strata corporation* in British Columbia and as the *co-proprietors* in Quebec) and the condominium council (referred to as the *strata council* in British Columbia). All condominium owners automatically become voting members of the condominium corporation. Normally, only one vote is given for each unit, regardless of the unit size or the number of owners of that unit.

The operation and management of a condominium development is similar to that of a company. In a company, those who own part of the company are shareholders, and collectively they control the company. Major decisions are voted on at the annual general meeting, and at the same meeting the board of directors is elected to run the day-by-day operations of the company on the shareholders' behalf. The condominium corporation performs a role similar to that of the shareholders in a company, while the condominium council operates much like a board of directors.

As you can see, there are a lot of controlling elements built into the condominium community structure in order to maintain consistency, continuity, and control for the betterment of all the members of the development. In addition to federal, provincial, and municipal government laws and regulations that impact on the development, there is in effect a fourth level of government. In many ways a condominium development may be similar to a self-contained and self-governed community. Naturally the bureaucratic nature and extent of this fourth level of government depends on its size, membership, and history.

An outline follows of common powers and duties of a condominium corporation and a condominium council. The exact duties and responsibilities can vary from province to province depending on the legislation and the original project documents or by-laws, and as mentioned, terminology can differ in each province; but the concepts are similar.

1. Condominium Corporation

(a) Powers

The condominium corporation has the power to:

- Purchase, hire, or otherwise acquire personal elements for use by owners in connection with their enjoyment of common property, common facilities, or other assets of the corporation.
- Borrow money required by it in the performance of its duties or the exercise of its powers.
- Secure the repayment of money borrowed by it, and the payment of interest, by negotiable instrument or mortgage of unpaid contributions, or mortgage of any property vested in it, or by a combination of those means.
- Invest as it may determine in separate accounts money in the fund for administrative expenses, or in the contingency reserve fund.
- Make an agreement with an owner or occupier of a unit for the provision of amenities or services by it to the unit or to the owner or occupier.
- Grant an owner the right to exclusive use and enjoyment of common elements, or special privileges for them, the grant to be determinable on reasonable notice.
- Designate an area as limited common elements and specify the units that are to have the use of the limited common elements.
- Make rules and regulations it considers necessary or desirable from time to time in relation to the enjoyment, safety, and cleanliness of the common elements, common facilities, or other assets of the corporation.
- Do all things necessary for the enforcement of the by-laws and the rules and regulations of the condominium corporation, and for the control, management, and administration of the common elements, common facilities, or other assets, including removing privileges in the use of certain facilities, or fixing and collecting fines for contravention of the by-laws, rules, or regulations.
- Determine the levy for the contingency reserve fund, which shall be not less than 5% (varies) of the total annual budget, until the reserve reaches an amount that the condominium council considers sufficient having regard to the type of buildings in the development, and thereafter raise further amounts of replacement funds from time to time.

- Join any organization serving the interests of condominium corporations and assess the membership fee in the organization as part of the common expenses.

(b) Duties

The condominium corporation must:

- Control, manage, and administer the common elements, common facilities, or other assets of the corporation for the benefit of all owners.
- Keep in a state of good and serviceable repair and properly maintain the fixtures and fittings—including the elevators, swimming pool, and recreational facilities, and other apparatus and equipment used in connection with the common elements, common facilities, or other assets of the corporation.
- Maintain all common areas, both internal and external, including lawns, gardens, parking and storage areas, public halls, and lobbies.
- Maintain and repair, including renewal where reasonably necessary, pipes, wires, cables, chutes, and ducts which are capable of being used in connection with the enjoyment of more than one unit or common elements.
- On the written request of an owner or mortgagee of a unit, produce the insurance policies effected by the corporation and the receipts for the last premiums.
- Maintain and repair the exterior of the buildings, excluding windows, doors, balconies, and patios included in a unit, but including the decorating of the whole of the exterior of the buildings.
- Collect and receive all contributions toward the common expenses paid by the owners and deposit the same with a savings institution.
- Pay all sums of money properly required to be paid on account of all services, supplies, and assessments pertaining to, or for the benefit of, the corporation.

2. Condominium Council

(a) Powers

The council has the power to:

- Meet for the conduct of business, and adjourn and otherwise regulate its meetings as it thinks fit. It shall meet when any member gives the other members not less than seven days' notice of a meeting proposed by him, specifying the reason for calling the meeting, unless the other members agree to waive the notice.
- Employ for and on behalf of the condominium corporation, agents and employees as it thinks proper for the control, management, and administration of the common property, common facilities, or other assets

of the corporation, and the exercise and performance of the powers and duties of the corporation.

- Delegate to one or more of its members, or to a member or committee of members of the condominium corporation, or to its manager, those of its powers and duties it thinks proper, and at any time revoke such a delegation.

(b) Duties

The council must keep, in one location, or in the possession of one person, and shall make available on request to an owner or a person authorized by him:

- A copy of the Condominium Act and changes in the by-laws
- A copy of special or unanimous resolutions
- A copy of all the legal agreements to which the corporation is a party, including management contracts, insurance policies, insurance trustee agreements, deeds, agreements for sale, leases, licences, easements, or rights of way
- A register of the members of the council
- A register of unit owners, setting out the unit number, the name of the owner, the unit entitlement, the name and address of any mortgagee who has notified the condominium corporation, the name of any tenant or lessee, and a notation of any assignment by the owner to the lessee
- The annual budget for each year
- Minutes of all general meetings and of all council meetings

The council must:

- Keep minutes of its proceedings
- Cause minutes to be kept of general meetings
- Cause proper books of account to be kept in respect of all sums of money received and expended by it and the matters in respect of which receipt and expenditure take place
- Prepare proper accounts relating to all money of the corporation, and the income and expenditure of it, for each annual general meeting
- On application of an owner or mortgagee, or a person authorized in writing by him, make the books of account available for inspection at all reasonable times

Because there are many duties which volunteer members of the condominium council do not have the time, skill, or inclination to fulfill, such as maintenance, repair, and the administration of routine matters, a management company is frequently hired under contract with the condominium corporation to deal with those tasks; or other procedures are set up to deal with routine matters. This is covered in the next section.

D. CONDOMINIUM MANAGEMENT

Many of the daily responsibilities of the condominium development are too time-consuming to be handled by the condominium council, especially considering that the council members are unpaid volunteers. The Condominium Act in most provinces permits the council to employ a professional management company to carry out these daily functions. The management company's authority and responsibility is limited to matters affecting the security and maintenance of the common elements, the assets, and the facilities of the condominium corporation. This limitation is to ensure that the management company does not take over the decision-making role of the council.

The initial decision regarding management is usually made by the owner/developer prior to any deal. The terms of the management contract, if any, and the relationship between the developer and the property manager, are required to be included in the original project documents that are filed in the land registry. The decision will be largely determined by the size of the project. Some larger developers have internal divisions which carry out the property management function. Under most Condominium Acts, the council can terminate the management contract established by the owner/developer within a certain period after the development is completed and registered or at the time that a certain percentage of the units are sold.

There are essentially three forms of condominium management: self-management, resident management, and professional management. A combination of these alternatives may also be employed.

1. Self-Management

In smaller condominium developments, it is often more practical for the owners to be responsible for the management of the development directly. For example, in a condominium duplex or development of up to approximately 15 units, this self-management alternative could be attractive. Another example would be a bare land condominium corporation which has minimal common elements and facilities to maintain. It is not necessary in a self-management situation that the owners themselves clean the grounds, cut the grass, do the gardening, and sweep the driveways. It does mean, though, that the owners, or a representative of the owners, would have to be directly involved in supervising the performance of these types of services. Frequently the jobs are done by volunteers, part-time or full-time employees, contracting firms, or combinations of this type of help, but for the sake of continuity and accurate delegation of responsibilities it is important that someone on council be responsible for communicating with those who are providing the services.

In addition to communicating with the staff, some form of supervision will have to be put into place to monitor such services as maintenance of the pool, grounds, and elevators, painting, garbage removal, and accounting and typing functions. Various federal and provincial government responsibilities relating to employees will also have to be considered, such as unemployment insurance, income tax deductions from employees' wages, and Workers' Compensation Board contributions. If the council negotiates with a contractor to provide services, then deductions do not have to be taken off in the same fashion as with employees, because the contractor would be signing a written agreement to the effect that they will hire and pay their own employees. In that event, the council would simply pay the negotiated contract fee for services rendered by the contractor.

Another reason for self-management is that a condominium development may be outside the metropolitan area, and so there may be difficulty in obtaining the services of a professional management company.

2. Resident Management

In this situation the condominium corporation employs one or more people directly to perform the daily management requirements. These people would normally operate out of an office in the development and would be paid a full-time or part-time salary. Because the manager would be an employee of the condominium corporation, he would in effect be an employee of all the owners; it is therefore important to be very careful in selecting the manager, in order to maintain harmony with the members. Generally only large condominium developments can financially justify employing a full-time resident manager.

3. Professional Management

Many condominium corporations use a professional management company to some extent. These companies tend to be experienced at condominium management and to have many systems and procedures for efficient operation of their support function. This would include computerized accounting procedures and management systems, experienced staff, access to suppliers who can provide bulk-buying discounts and good service, and careful selection of competent tradesmen. One of the key benefits of using a professional management company is that due to the periodic turnover of council members, such a company will provide the continuity of management to ensure a consistent level of quality in the condominium development. The responsibility of the condominium council would be one of providing instructions to the management company and monitoring the company's performance.

E. DUTIES AND RESPONSIBILITIES OF A CONDOMINIUM OWNER

A condominium owner has certain legal duties and responsibilities arising out of the owning of a condominium and being a member of a condominium corporation. Although the duties and responsibilities can vary from development to development and from province to province, most of the legal requirements cover the same general topic areas and are outlined in the by-laws and the rules and regulations. The following are examples of typical by-laws relating to the responsibilities of the condominium owner.

The owner must:

- Permit the condominium corporation and its agents, at all reasonable times on notice, except in case of emergency when no notice is required, to enter his unit for the purpose of inspecting, repairing, and maintaining pipes, wires, cables, ducts, or other common assets of the condominium corporation within the unit.
- Promptly carry out all work that may be ordered by any competent public or local authority in respect of his unit other than work for the benefit of the building generally, and pay all rates, taxes, charges, and assessments that may be payable in respect of his unit.
- Repair and maintain his unit, including windows and doors, and areas allocated to his exclusive use, and keep them in a good state of repair.
- Use and enjoy the common elements, common facilities, or other assets of the condominium corporation in a manner that will not unreasonably interfere with their use and enjoyment by other owners, their families, or visitors.
- Not use his unit, or permit it to be used, for a purpose that will cause a nuisance or hazard to any occupier of a unit, whether an owner or not.
- Notify the condominium corporation promptly on any change of ownership or of any mortgage or other dealing in connection with his unit.
- Comply strictly with the by-laws of the condominium corporation, and with the rules and regulations as adopted from time to time.
- Receive the written permission of the condominium council before undertaking alterations to the exterior or structure of the unit.
- Pay his share of the common expenses established by the condominium corporation, including any special assessments.
- Pay his share of any judgement registered against the common elements. *Note:* This liability arises because the unit owner owns a share of the common elements as a tenant in common. For this reason owners should be aware of the extent of liability insurance arranged by the condominium corporation.

F. EXPENSES RELATING TO CONDOMINIUM OWNERSHIP

Once you have completed the purchase transaction, and you are now an owner of a condominium unit, there are ongoing monthly or annual expenses and potential expenses that you have to plan for. The most common expenses are as follows.

1. Mortgage Payments

Unless you paid cash for your unit, you will be making monthly payments for principal, interest, and probably taxes. Details on financing a condominium by obtaining a mortgage are covered in Chapter 3.

2. Property Taxes

Each individual condominium unit is assessed by the municipality and has to make annual payment for the property taxes. If you have a mortgage, the lender may or may not have required you to include extra monthly payments along with your mortgage. These are held in a property tax account so that the lender can pay for your municipal property taxes annually. If you do not have a mortgage you will have to pay property tax separately. The common elements have a property tax as well, but that tax is covered in your monthly maintenance payments.

3. Maintenance Payments

Maintenance payments or "assessments for common expenses" cover all the operating costs of the common elements and are adjusted accordingly for any increase or decrease in expenses. You are responsible for a portion of the development's total operating cost. The formula for determining your portion will be discussed shortly. The payments for common expenses are made directly to the condominium corporation and generally cover the following items.

(a) Maintenance and Repair of Common Property
This includes costs for maintenance, landscaping, building repairs, recreational facilities, equipment, and other expenses.

(b) Operating and Service Costs
This includes expenses relating to garbage removal, heat, hydro, and electricity.

(c) Contingency Reserve Fund
This is a fund for unforeseen problems and expenses (for example, the roof needing replacement or the swimming pool or heating system breaking down). This fund is for expenses that have not been included in the

annual budgeted expense calculations for the common property and other assets of the condominium corporation. Owners contribute monthly to this fund, on the basis of a portion of the monthly maintenance fee. The condominium legislation in most provinces requires a minimum amount to be contributed to the contingency reserve fund (e.g., 10% of annual budget). If you are buying an older condominium, you should check to see what percentage of the monthly payments is being allocated toward this fund, as there is a higher risk of needing to use the fund in older buildings than in new developments. In older buildings, the fund should possibly be 25% or more, depending on the circumstances. In most cases you are not entitled to a refund of your contribution to the reserve fund when you sell your unit.

(d) Management Costs

These are the costs associated with hiring private individuals or professional management firms to administer all or part of the daily functions of the condominium development.

(e) Insurance

Condominium legislation requires that the development carry sufficient fire and related insurance to replace the common property in the event of fire or other damage. Condominium corporations generally obtain further insurance to cover other payables and liabilities. The insurance does not cover the damage done to the interior of an individual unit.

4. Special Assessment

There could be situations in which there is desire by 75% or more of the condominium members to raise funds for special purposes. These funds would not be able to come from the contingency reserve fund or from the regular monthly assessments. For example, there could be an interest in building a swimming pool or tennis courts, or it may be necessary to cover costs of repairs beyond the contingency reserve fund. Once the decision is made to assess members, you cannot refuse to pay the special assessment if it has been properly approved, even though you might not agree with its purpose.

5. Condominium Owner Insurance

As mentioned earlier, the insurance on the building that is covered by the condominium development does not include the interior of your unit. Therefore, you will need to get separate insurance to cover the contents as well as damage to the inside of your unit, including walls, windows, and doors. There are several types of possible insurance, including replacement-cost, all-risk comprehensive, and personal liability. It is also common to get insurance to cover deficiencies in the condominium corporation's insurance coverage in the event of fire so that any damage to your unit could be repaired in full; otherwise the unit owners would have to pay on a proportional basis any deficiency by means of a special assessment. Many insurance companies have developed a specialized program referred to as *condominium home owner's package* insurance. Check in the Yellow Pages under "Insurance Brokers" and compare coverages and costs.

6. Lease Payments

If you have a leasehold condominium, you will be required to make monthly lease payments in addition to many of the other costs outlined in this section.

7. Utilities

You are responsible for your own utilities that you use in your unit, including hydro, water, heat, etc. In apartment condominiums these expenses are usually included in the maintenance fee, whereas townhouse condominiums tend to be separately metered and you are billed directly and individually by the utility companies.

8. Unit Repair and Maintenance Costs

You will have to allocate a certain amount of your personal financial budget to repair and maintenance needs relating to the inside of your unit. Your monthly assessment fee would cover common elements outside your unit only.

Unit entitlement is the basis on which the owner's contribution to the common expenses or maintenance fees of the condominium corporation are calculated. Various formulas are used for the calculation. In some developments the percentage calculated for the unit's share is determined by the original purchase price of each unit in relation to the value of the total property. Another method is to apportion costs on the basis of the number of units in equal proportion, regardless of unit size. But the most common formula is to calculate the unit entitlement by dividing the number of square feet in an owner's unit by the number of square feet in all the units. For example, let's say a condominium development contains 15 condominium units, the total square feet of all units is 15,680, your individual unit is 784 square feet, and the annual cost to maintain the common elements and other related expenses is $40,000. Then to calculate your monthly financial commitment you would go through the following steps:

- Calculate the unit entitlement (784 ÷ 15,680 = 1/20 share in the common property)

- Calculate the annual share of maintenance costs ($1/20 \times \$40,000 =$ $2,000 per year)
- Calculate the monthly share of maintenance costs ($1/12 \times \$2,000 =$ $166.66 per month)

G. DEALING WITH CONDOMINIUM DISPUTES

In the condominium community there is always a possibility of having a problem or a dispute that may not be able to be resolved quickly and easily. It is important to know your rights and options in that event. This section will cover the most common types of disputes and the means of resolving those disputes.

1. Nature of Common Disputes

Problems tend to fall into the following general categories:

(a) The Five *p*'s: Pets, Parking, Parties, People, Personalities

The five *p*'s tend to be the most common areas of annoyance. Common complaints are: *Pets* are noisy, roaming, scaring children, or fouling the common property. *Parking spaces* are being used by members or guests in a consistently selfish and irresponsible fashion. *People* and *parties* are too loud for too long at too-late hours. *Personalities* may become a problem because of the close proximity of the community environment; some owners get annoyed by people using or abusing the common elements, and some people have a tendency to irritate others by virtue of their attitude, arrogance, indifference, or discourtesy.

(b) Decisions of the Condominium Corporation or Council

Examples of disputes in this area are: you believe that the conduct of the corporation or council is oppressive and unfairly prejudicial to your rights; you believe that a decision relating to a special assessment was unnecessary and irresponsible; you were fined for allegedly breaching the by-laws or rules and regulations and you believe the fine was unfair and unwarranted.

2. Resolution of Disputes

The means for the resolution of disputes, in ascending order of complexity, are: negotiation, mediation, arbitration, and litigation.

(a) Negotiation

It is always best to attempt to resolve the dispute by discussing the matter directly with the person concerned. That may be all that is necessary to resolve the problem. It is worthwhile to at least attempt that first step.

(b) Mediation

If the first step is not successful, you may wish to contact the condominium council and make a complaint to them outlining your dispute. If the conduct of another owner has contravened the by-laws or rules and regulations, it would be helpful to draw those points to the attention of the council. The council has the authority in most cases to deal with infringements of the by-laws or rules and regulations.

(c) Arbitration

If your attempts to have a dispute resolved through using the condominium council have not been successful, you may wish to consider arbitration. Condominium legislation of most provinces sets out the procedures for the arbitration process. Normally the process is not available if litigation has commenced. Matters that may require arbitration include disputes about: contributions to common expenses; fines for breach of by-laws or rules and regulations; damages to common elements, common facilities, and other assets of the condominium corporation; and decisions of the council or the corporation.

The parties should agree on a single arbitrator, but if that is not possible, each party selects its own arbitrator and the two arbitrators select a third who acts as a chairman. Unless the parties otherwise agree, each arbitrator generally must be an owner and occupier of a condominium unit in another development for at least one year, but may not be a member of the condominium corporation affected by the arbitration. The arbitrators may accept evidence under oath and may make whatever decision they consider just and equitable. The arbitrators' decision is entered into court as if it was an order of the court. The process just described is a common procedure set out in most provincial Condominium Acts, although the procedures may vary in individual provinces.

A list of arbitrators is available upon request from most professional condominium management companies. Another option is to contact the Canadian Condominium Institute (CCI), based in Toronto. The CCI has branches in various provinces throughout Canada and a network of arbitrators that are available for resolution of disputes. The contact address for CCI is located in Appendix A, "Sources of Further Information."

(d) Litigation

If all else fails, you have rights in common law, as well as under most provincial condominium legislation, to commence action in court. You can proceed against a condominium corporation or council to rectify what you believe is a failure to meet their obligations under the Condominium Act or by-laws or because you feel that actions toward you have been oppressive. The court can make any order it considers appropriate depending on the circumstances.

The difficulty in the litigation process, of course, is the fact that it can be very expensive, stressful, uncertain, and lengthy. If you have a problem that you are concerned about and want to decide whether you should go the arbitration or the litigation route, you should seek a legal opinion from a lawyer who specializes in condominium law. Ideally it would be helpful to obtain a second opinion from another lawyer who specializes in condominium law in order to satisfy yourself that the advice you are getting and intend to rely on is consistent. How to select a lawyer is covered in Chapter 2.

H. SELECTING THE RIGHT CONDOMINIUM FOR YOUR NEEDS

Selecting the right condominium can be a stressful and frustrating experience, as with any real estate search. It makes it easier if you have methodically prepared for the process by understanding the marketplace and your own needs and knowing the features to look for. Choosing a suitable real estate agent is an important step at this stage. That issue, too, is covered in Chapter 2.

1. Understanding Market Conditions

It is helpful to understand the nature of home buying market conditions that impact on the availability, selection, and price of the type of condominium that you are looking for. There are three types of markets: the seller's market, the buyer's market, and the balanced market.

(a) Seller's Market
In a seller's market the number of buyers wanting homes exceeds the supply or number of homes on the market. This type of market is characterized by homes that sell quickly, an increase in prices, a large number of buyers, and a minimal inventory of homes. These characteristics have implications for the buyer, who has to make decisions quickly, must pay more, and frequently has his conditional offers rejected.

(b) Buyer's Market
In a buyer's market the supply of homes on the market exceeds the demand or number of buyers. Characteristics of this type of market include: homes being on the market longer, fewer buyers compared to availability, higher inventory of homes, and stabilized prices or a reduction in prices. The implications for buyers in this type of market are: more favourable negotiating leverage and more time to search for a home.

(c) Balanced Market
In a balanced market the number of homes on the market is equal to the demand or number of buyers. The characteristics of this type of market include: houses selling within a reasonable period, demand equalling

supply, sellers accepting reasonable offers, and prices generally stabilized. The implications for the buyer of this type of market are that the atmosphere is more relaxed and there is a reasonable number of homes to choose from.

2. Understanding Your Own Needs

A detailed assessment of your personal and family needs is very important. This would include your short-, medium-, and long-term needs with regard to type of accommodation, financial capacity to debt-service the condominium, the location relative to commuting requirements and other needs, and input from other family members who will be living in the condominium with you. Speaking to friends or business associates who currently live or who have lived in a condominium and obtaining their perspective would be helpful. As mentioned at the beginning of this chapter, the condominium concept is not for everyone, and a review of the advantages and disadvantages outlined earlier would be a helpful starting point.

3. General Features to Look For

Checklist 1 at the end of this book sets out many of the features that you should consider and compare in condominiums that interest you. Some of the general features are discussed below.

(a) Location

One of the prime considerations is the location. How close is the condominium to schools, cultural attractions, shopping centres, recreational facilities, work, and transportation? How attractive is the present and future development of the area surrounding the condominium? (You could move into a condominium unit, and six months later, a high-rise condominium complex could be built across from you, blocking your view and therefore decreasing the resale value of your unit.) The location should have ample access to parking and other attractive features. Check on the amount of traffic on the streets in the area. Heavy traffic can be a noise nuisance as well as a hazard for young children.

(b) Privacy

Privacy is an important consideration and has to be thoroughly explored. For example, you want to make sure that the sound insulation between the walls and floors and ceiling of your unit is sufficient to enable you to live comfortably without annoying your neighbours or having your neighbours annoy you. If you have a townhouse unit, such factors as the distance between your unit and other common areas, including walkways, roads, and fences, are important.

(c) Noise

Thoroughly check the level of noise. Consider such factors as location of highways, driveways, parking lots, playgrounds, garage doors, elevators, garbage chutes, and the heating and air conditioning plant or equipment.

(d) Pricing

The pricing of the condominium you are considering should be competitive with that of other, similar offerings. On the other hand, it is sometimes difficult to compare prices accurately without taking into account the different amenities that may be available in one condominium that are not available in the other—tennis courts, swimming pool, recreation centre, etc. You may decide that you do not want these extra facilities in view of your lifestyle needs, in which case paying an extra price for the unit because of these features would not be attractive.

(e) Common Elements and Facilities

Review all the common elements that make up the condominium development. Consider them from the perspective of the relevance to your needs as well as the maintenance or operational costs that might be required to service these features.

(f) Storage Facilities

Check out the type of storage space available, including its location and size. Does there appear to be sufficient storage space for your needs, or will you have to rent a mini-locker to store excess items?

(g) Parking Facilities

Are the facilities outdoors or underground? Do you feel there is sufficient lighting for security protection? Is it a long distance from the parking spot to your home? Is there parking space available for a boat, trailer, or second car, and is there ample visitor parking?

(h) Quality of Construction Materials

Thoroughly look at your unit and the surrounding development in an attempt to make an assessment of the overall quality of the development. Keep in mind that you are responsible for paying a portion of the maintenance costs for the common elements. You may wish to hire a contractor whom you trust to give you an opinion on the quality and condition of the construction before committing yourself by signing the formal agreement for purchase and sale.

(i) Design and Layout of Unit

When looking at the unit, consider your present and future needs. Although you are entitled to use the interior of your unit as you wish, there are restrictions relating to the exterior of your unit or any structural changes that you may make to the unit. If you are intending to have a separate room for an expanded family, inlaws, or an office, you should consider the implications beforehand. For example, you may find that the patio is very windy and you would like to have a solarium built to enclose the patio for that reason. There is a very good chance that you would not be able to do so without the consent of the condominium council, because it would affect the exterior appearance of the development.

(j) Property Taxes

Compare the costs of taxes in the area that you are considering with those of other areas equally attractive to you. Different municipalities have different tax rates and there could be a considerable cost saving or expense. Also enquire as to whether there is any anticipated tax increase and why.

(k) Neighbours

Look at the surrounding neighbourhood and make an assessment as to whether the value of the residences in the neighbourhood will affect the value of your condominium. For example, are the homes in the area well maintained? Are there children in the same age group as your own children?

(l) Owner/Occupiers vs. Tenants

Ask how many tenants, as opposed to owners, there will be in the condominium, and the maximum number of tenants allowed. The higher the percentage of owner/occupiers, the better the chance that there will be more pride of ownership and therefore more responsible treatment of common elements and amenities.

(m) Mix of Other Owners in the Development

Check to see the type of people who are also living in the development. Are they single adults, young couples—with or without children?—or older/retired people?

(n) Condominium Management

Enquire as to whether the development is going to be operated by a professional management company, operated by a resident manager, or self-managed. Ideally, you should check out the condominium unit that you are interested in at three different times: during the day, in the evening, and on the weekend. That should give you a better profile of noise factors, children, or parties.

I. SELLING A CONDOMINIUM

The legal aspects of selling a condominium, selecting a realtor and signing a listing agreement are covered in Chapter 2. This section deals with the marketing techniques to make your home more attractive to a prospective buyer or at an open house. Your real estate agent will provide you with more information and advice. The following steps should assist your agent in selling your home at the best possible price and as quickly as possible. Most of the examples relate to any condominium, although some of them, as noted, are specific to the townhouse type.

(a) Keep Things Clean

Keep windows sparkling and clean, inside and outside. Have drapes, carpets, and rugs cleaned and vacuumed. Keep front and back entrances clear, clean, and inviting.

(b) Make the Interior Decorating Attractive

Major decorating before selling may be neither necessary nor desirable because many buyers will probably prefer to select their own paints and colours. A dingy closet or a badly marked wall can be made much more attractive with a good scrub, a touch of fresh paint, or a bright strip of wallpaper.

(c) Unclutter the Premises

Keep untidiness to a minimum. Rooms can look comfortable and lived in without being untidy. Vacuum and dust thoroughly. Keep kitchen and bathroom counters gleaming, tables uncluttered, and dirty dishes out of sight. Clean up books and magazines and clothes that might be lying around in a messy fashion. Move out excess furniture if it makes the unit look cluttered and small with little floor space.

(d) Clean Up All Closets

Make the best use of space. Show your closet and storage areas off to their best advantage. Linens should be stacked neatly; hang clothes carefully; use garment bags and shoe racks. Crammed closets look small, but well-organized ones appear larger than they really are.

(e) Make Kitchens and Bathrooms Inviting

The two most important rooms to many buyers are the kitchen and the bathroom. It is particularly important to make those areas appealing. Keep both rooms immaculately tidy and spotlessly clean. You want to create the impression that the home is easy to maintain.

(f) Tidy Up the Garage (Townhouse Condominium)

Keep your garage or carport neat and organized to show all the extra storage space. A garage can be a selling point, particularly if viewers are accustomed to the parking or storage problems associated with apartment living.

(g) Maintain Your Landscaping (Townhouse Condominium)

Keep your lawn, shrubs, and garden tidy and trimmed.

(h) Make Necessary Repairs

You may be accustomed to a broken window catch, dripping tap, or sticking or squeaky door, but potential buyers will notice and develop a negative impression.

(i) Make the Home as Peaceful as Possible

Keep noise to a minimum to let prospective buyer and real estate agent examine your home without distraction. Quiet music in the background might have a pleasant effect, but noisy children or TV or stereo sounds can annoy prospective buyers.

(j) Provide a Comfortable Environment

Make sure the unit is at a comfortable temperature: fresh and airy on hot summer days and warm during cold days. The right number of lights should be turned on after dark, and a crackling fire presents a homey feeling on a fall or winter evening. Freshly cut flowers in various rooms such as the kitchen, living room, dining room, bathroom, and master bedroom would be inviting. The delicious smell of baking coming from the kitchen can be appealing and make one feel at home. Be cautious about cooking, though, as some cooking odours can be quite offensive and linger for a long time.

(k) Keep Pets Out of the Way

Buyers may not enjoy being welcomed by a cat or dog. Some people are allergic to animals and others don't like them. Many people could be turned off by knowing that various animals have resided in the home.

The preceding hints are simply basic guidelines to remind you how important it is to set the correct mood and environment for a buyer to want to buy your condominium. The best approach is to try to see your home through the eyes of a buyer in terms of what would attract *you*.

J. INVESTING IN A CONDOMINIUM

The first-time real estate investor could find buying a condominium unit as a rental property an attractive option for several reasons. If you are considering investing in a condominium, it is important to consider the advantages and disadvantages of the different types of condominiums, for example, apartment, conversion, or townhouse. Check on whether rental units are permitted in the development, and on the current mix of tenants and owner/occupiers.

Here are some of the benefits you may wish to consider:

- Condominiums generally appreciate in value at a rate which is almost consistently higher than the inflation rate.

- Finding an occupant for a condominium apartment is relatively easy in many major Canadian cities because of low vacancy rates.
- There is an increasing demand for the condominium lifestyle and the luxury and convenience that it provides.
- Because a minimal amount of upkeep is involved, the economic benefits are more attractive for the first-time investor.
- There is the convenience of having many of the management and maintenance problems taken care of by the condominium corporation, and the professional management company if any.
- Facilities such as tennis courts and swimming pools are maintained by the condominium corporation, thereby freeing the new investor from the responsibilities of upkeep.
- The owner is protected by the by-laws and the rules and regulations set by provincial condominium legislation, by the original project documents, or by the condominium council. For example, many condominiums do not allow pets in the building because of the potential wear and tear on the apartment. This type of rule protects and benefits the investor.

If you are looking for higher appreciation (resale value), the purchase of the least expensive unit in a luxury condominium/townhouse complex generally offers a more financially attractive return than the purchase of the largest unit in a modestly priced development, assuming the price is the same. Your research will provide you with the necessary background statistics in your market interest area.

If you decide to invest in a condominium rental property, many of your personal expenses may be deducted from income in addition to the normal tax deductions such as mortgage, interest, depreciation, and other condominium-related expenses. For example, you would normally be entitled to set up a small office in your current residence for managing your investments, which would include keeping your records. You could deduct a percentage of all your home-related expenses. The normal formula is to take the square footage of the office area that you are using relative to the total square footage in your home. In general terms, 10 to 15% is usually deducted for that portion. In addition, you would be entitled to deduct a part of the car-related expenses involved in managing your investment portfolio, whether it be one rental property or more than one. The percentage of all your car-related expenses can vary, obviously depending on the usage of the car relating to your investment.

If you are seriously contemplating investing in a condominium, it is important to seek competent tax and accounting advice and legal advice from a lawyer specializing in condominium law.

CHAPTER

2

Legal Aspects

INTRODUCTION

There are many legal considerations connected with purchasing a condominium that are in addition to and distinct from those connected with purchasing a conventional house. Some of these have been briefly covered in the previous chapter and are mentioned in other chapters of this book. It is important to have an understanding of the issues and terminology in order to discuss the appropriate matters clearly with your lawyer and make the correct decisions.

This chapter explains the kinds of property ownership, understanding the legal documents involved in a purchase and sale, selecting a lawyer, the services provided by a lawyer, selecting a realtor, and types of listing agreements.

A. TYPES OF OWNERSHIP OF PROPERTY

1. Types of Interest in Land

There are several types of legal interests in land, the most common being freehold and leasehold.

(a) Freehold
This type of ownership in land entitles the owner to use the land for an indefinite period of time and to deal with the land in any way he wishes, subject to legislation (for example, the Condominium Act), contractual obligations (for example, declaration, rules and regulations, etc.) and any charges which encumber the title of the property and which are filed in

the provincial land registry office (e.g., mortgages, liens, judgements, etc.). Another term for freehold is *fee simple*. Fee simple ownership of property is referred to as an "indefeasible" title. Most owners of condominiums acquire fee simple interest.

(b) Leasehold Interest

In this example the holder of the interest in land has the right to use the land for a fixed period of time, for example, 50 or 99 years. The owner of the property (landlord or lessor) signs an agreement with the owner of the leasehold interest (tenant or lessee) setting out various terms and conditions of the relationship. The contract in relation to a condominium would set out such conditions as maintenance requirements, restrictions on use of the land, building construction requirements, and other matters. The leasehold interest can be bought and sold, but the leaseholder can only sell the right to use the land for the time that is remaining in the lease—subject, of course, to any conditions contained in the original lease.

Both freehold interest and leasehold interest can be left in your will as an asset of your estate or specifically bequeathed in your will.

2. Types of Joint Ownership in Property

You may wish to have shared ownership in the property with one or more other persons. There are two main types of joint ownership: joint tenancy and tenancy in common.

(a) Joint Tenancy

This is a situation in which an owner has an undivided but equal share with all the other owners. No one person has a part of the property of which he can say it specifically is his, because all the property belongs to all of the owners. At the time of purchase of the property, all the people who are joint tenants will show up on the title of the property equally and each of the joint tenants has the rights in law to possession of the whole property. These are the essential conditions involved in joint tenancy, and if any of these conditions are not met, then the ownership is deemed to be a tenancy in common and not joint tenancy. The title of the property will list all the parties' names and will clearly state that they are joint tenants.

If it does not specifically state joint tenancy on the title, the situation is generally deemed to be tenancy in common. And you can easily terminate your joint tenancy relationship by simply mortgaging or selling your interest to one of the other joint tenants or to another party. For example, if there are three joint tenants, you would be selling or mortgaging 1/3 of the property. The act of mortgaging or selling your interest immediately creates a tenancy in common in most cases.

One of the main features of a joint tenancy is the right of survivorship. This means that if one of the joint tenants dies, the others automatically and immediately receive the deceased person's share, equally divided. In other words, the deceased person's share in the joint tenancy is not passed on as an asset of his or her estate to beneficiaries, whether or not a will exists. It is fairly common for a couple to hold the legal interest in the property by means of joint tenancy. Thus, you should consider tenancy in common if you do not want to have your interest go automatically to the other parties.

(b) Tenancy in Common

In this form of ownership, the tenants can hold unequal shares in the property. Each party owns an undivided share in the property and therefore is entitled to possession of the whole of the property. For example, there could be five people who are tenants in common, but four of them could own 1/10 of the property each, and the fifth person own 6/10 of the property.

If the holder of a tenancy in common wishes to sell or mortgage his interest in the property, that can be done. When a buyer cannot be found and the tenant in common wants to obtain his money out of the property, he can go to court and under a legal procedure called *partition* request that the court order the property be sold and that it distribute the net proceeds of sale proportionately.

Tenancy in common does not carry an automatic right of survivorship as in joint tenancy. In other words, if one of the tenants in common dies, the interest does not go to the other tenants, but goes to the estate of the deceased. If there is a will, it is distributed under the terms of the will. If the deceased person does not have a will, there is provincial legislation dealing with that type of situation, and the person's assets, which would include the tenancy interest, would be distributed to relatives according to the legislation.

There are various reasons why some people prefer tenancy in common to joint tenancy. For example, if you are purchasing property with people who are not relatives, you would not want them to automatically have your interest in the property in the event of your death. Another reason why people prefer a tenancy in common is that if they have been previously married and they have children from a previous relationship, they may want to specify in their will that a certain portion of the worth of the estate goes to those children individually or collectively. The only way this can be dealt with is in a tenancy-in-common situation, because the interest would be deemed to be an asset of one's estate. Another reason why people may prefer a tenancy in common is that they are putting unequal amounts of money into the property, and a tenancy-in-common structure would reflect those different contributions in terms of the percentage interest in the property.

Written agreements are frequently signed by tenants in common setting out the procedures if one of them wants out of the situation. This can be done by giving the others the first right of refusal on a proportional basis to buy out the interest; or there could be a clause requiring the consent of the other tenants in common in approving of a potential purchaser; or there could be a provision requiring a certain period of notice to the other tenants before the property is sold. Another case when tenancy in common might be preferable would be when one of the owners of the property wishes to have the personal independence to raise money for other, outside interests, for example a business. The tenancy-in-common portion could be mortgaged without the consent of the other parties. In the case of resort condominium timeshares, the tenancy-in-common legal format, along with other contractual documentation, is the common method by which the interest is held. This is covered in more detail in the chapter on timeshares (Chapter 4).

B. UNDERSTANDING THE PURCHASE AND SALE AGREEMENT

The most important document you will sign will be the offer to purchase, which if accepted becomes the agreement of purchase and sale. It sets out the terms and conditions between the parties and, as in any contract, it is legally binding if no conditions exist in the contract that have to be met before it becomes binding. (Of course, there can be verbal contracts, but all contracts dealing with land must be in writing to be enforceable. That includes the purchase and sale agreement or a lease, which of course is also a contract.)

This section will cover the elements that make up a contract, legal implications of backing out of the agreement, and how to understand the contents of a purchase and sale agreement.

1. Elements of a Contract

Five main elements have to be present in order for a contract to be valid. These are: mutual agreement, legal capacity, exchange of consideration, intention to be bound, and compliance with the law.

(a) Mutual Agreement
There must be an offer and an acceptance. The terms and conditions of the bargain must be specific, complete, clear, and unambiguous. The parties to the contract must be sufficiently identifiable.

An offer may be withdrawn (revoked) any time before acceptance by the other party, as long as that revocation is transmitted, ideally in writing, to the other party. If the offer has already been accepted without condition and signed to that effect before receipt of the revokation, a binding contract has occurred.

(b) Legal Capacity

The parties to a contract must have the capacity to enter into a legally binding contract; otherwise the contract cannot be enforced. Each party to a contract:

- Must be an adult—i.e., over the "age of majority," which varies from province to province but is usually 19 years or older
- Must not have impaired judgement—i.e., the party must understand the nature and quality of what is involved in signing the contract; if a person is impaired by drugs, alcohol, stroke, or mental infirmity (diminished capacity), that would invalidate the contract if it could be proven
- Must not be insane in medical and legal terms
- Must be able to act with free will—i.e., is not under duress or threat or intimidation

(c) Exchange of Consideration

This concept means that something of value must be exchanged by the parties in order to bind the contract. Usually, money changes hands, but "consideration" could mean another house by exchange, something of value to the other side such as a service or product or other benefit, or a promise to do something in exchange for a promise to do something.

(d) Intention to Be Bound

The parties must have the intention of being bound by the agreement and its commitments, and must expect that it will be a bargain that could be enforced by the courts.

(e) Compliance with the Law

A contract, to be enforceable, must be legal in its purpose and intent. The courts will not enforce a contract which is intended to, or has the effect of, breaching federal, provincial, or municipal legislation.

2. Legal Options and Implications of Getting Out of a Signed Contract

There are instances wherein either the vendor or the purchaser may wish to back out of the agreement. Some examples are discussed below.

(a) Recision

In many provinces of Canada and states in the United States there is a "cooling-off" or recision period whereby the purchaser of a *new* condominium has a period of time (usually from three days to thirty days) to back out of the contract by giving notice to the vendor in writing before the deadline. The vendor is obliged to pay all the money back without penalty that the purchaser has placed on deposit. In cases where legislation does not give an automatic right to recision, the documents which are a part of the condominium package may have a recision period built in. If you do not have a statutory right to recision and it is not part of the documents relating to the purchase of a new condominium, then you may want to make it a condition of your offer.

(b) Specific Performance

If the vendor or purchaser refuses to go through with a purchase and sale agreement when there are no conditions attached to the agreement, the other party is entitled to go to court and request the court to order that the breaching party specifically perform the terms of the agreement, i.e., complete the transaction.

(c) Damages

If one party refuses to complete the agreement, instead of suing for specific performance of the terms of the agreement, the other party can sue for damages. Damages mean the financial losses which have been incurred because the other party failed to complete the bargain. In general terms, you have to prove damages to obtain damages. For example, if a vendor refused to complete the deal because he thought he could make $50,000 more on the sale of the house—the prices having gone up considerably— and if in fact it could be shown that he did sell it for $50,000 more after refusing to go through with your signed commitment, then you could claim $50,000 damages. Your loss could be quantified, assuming that there were not other reasons that could explain the differential in price. Alternatively, if the purchaser fails to complete and the vendor can show that he was relying on those funds and therefore that the purchase he had planned failed to occur, and so on down the line with various back-to-back purchases and sales that were all relying on the first, there could be considerable damages for which the purchaser can be sued.

(d) Conditional Contract

If the vendor or purchaser has preliminary conditions built into the purchase and sale agreement and those conditions cannot be met and therefore block the deal at the outset, no valid binding contract exists and neither party is liable to the other.

(e) Void Contracts

A contract is void and unenforceable if the required elements that make up a contract are not present, or if the contract is prohibited by statute.

(f) Voidable Contracts

If one of the parties has been induced into entering the contract on the basis of misrepresentation, whether innocent, negligent, or fraudulent, that party may be entitled to void the contract. If the misrepresentation was innocent, generally the contract can only be cancelled and any money returned, and no damages can be recovered in court. If there is negligent or fraudulent misrepresentation, however, not only can the contract be cancelled, but damages can also be recovered in court. For example, if the vendor was going to provide vendor-back financing and relied on representations of the purchaser concerning his creditworthiness and ability to pay, and prior to completion of the transaction, by doing a credit check and/or other investigation, the vendor finds out that the purchaser is a terrible credit risk, then that could be deemed to be negligent or fraudulent misrepresentation and the contract could be cancelled for that reason. To give another example, if the purchaser finds out before completion that the representation of the vendor or the vendor's agent is grossly untrue (for example, that zoning has been approved for subdivision purposes, and investigation shows that no application has been made for subdivision purposes), then the purchaser could get out of the contract and sue to recover damages, if any can be proven.

These are just some illustrations of the types of factors that could impact on the validity or enforceability of the contract. You can see how competent legal advice from a skilled real estate lawyer is necessary to minimize potential problems.

3. Understanding the Purchase and Sale Agreement

Most purchase and sale agreements come in standard formats, with standard clauses, and are drafted by the builder, the local real estate board, or commercial stationers, though there are generally spaces throughout the agreement for additional, customized clauses to be added. A contract prepared by a builder has distinctly different clauses from those of a standard form for resales, and there are considerable differences in the standard contract clauses between builders and between real estate boards.

There is a high risk that the standard clauses, or additional ones that you may choose to insert, will not be comprehensive enough for your needs; you may not even understand them or the implications of them— and sign the agreement regardless. That is why it is so important to have a lawyer review your offer to purchase *before* you sign it. Regrettably, only a small percentage of people do this, because they either don't realize they should, perceive it will be an unnecessary or costly legal expense, or are naive or too trusting. It would be false economy to save on a legal consultation, as the costs to obtain a legal opinion are very reasonable relative to the risk involved in signing a bad contract. Alternatively, rather than seeing a lawyer before submitting an offer to purchase, some people may wish to insert a condition that states the offer is "subject to approval as to form and contents by the purchaser's solicitor, such approval to be communicated to vendor within x days of acceptance, or to be deemed to be withheld."

There are many common clauses and features contained in the purchase and sale agreement, many of which vary from contract to contract according to various circumstances—whether one is purchasing a new or a resale condominium, etc. A brief overview follows of some of the common features of the agreement for purchase and sale.

(a) Amount of Deposit

A deposit serves various purposes. It is a partial payment on the purchase price, a good-faith indication of seriousness, and an assurance of performance if all the conditions in the offer to purchase have been fulfilled. The deposit is generally 5 to 10% of the purchase price. If there were conditions in the offer, and these conditions were not met, then the purchaser is entitled to receive the full amount of the deposit back. This is one reason why it is important to have conditions or "subject to" clauses in the offer to protect one's interests fully. Most agreements for purchase and sale have a provision that gives the vendor the option of keeping the deposit as "liquidated damages" in the event that the purchaser fails to complete the terms of the agreement and pay the balance of money on the closing date.

When making a deposit, it is very important to be careful whom the funds are paid to. If you are purchasing on a private sale and no realtor is involved, never pay the funds directly to the vendor; pay them to your own lawyer in trust. If a realtor is involved, the funds can be paid to the realtor's trust account or your own lawyer's trust account as the situation dictates. If you are purchasing a new condominium from the builder, do not pay a deposit directly to the builder. The money should go to your lawyer's trust account, or some other system should be set up for your protection ensuring that your funds cannot be used except under certain conditions based on those which are clearly set out in the agreement. Or you might get insurance protection for your funds. The risk is high in paying your money to a developer, because if the developer does not complete the project and goes into bankruptcy, you could lose all your money, and in practical terms could have great difficulty getting it back. Though most provincial governments have brought in legislation dealing with new condominium projects to protect the public on the issue of deposits—as well as many other condominium risk areas—legislation provides only partial protection.

Another matter you have to consider is interest. If you are paying a deposit, you want to ensure that interest at the appropriate rate or based on the appropriate formula is paid to your credit. In many cases, deposit monies can be tied up for many months, and that could represent considerable interest.

(b) Conditions and Warranties

It is important to understand the distinction between *conditions* and *warranties*, as it is very critical to the wording that you would be using in the agreement. A *condition* is a requirement which is fundamental to the very existence of the offer. A breach of condition allows the buyer to get out of the contract and obtain the full amount of the deposit back. An inability to meet the condition set by a vendor permits the vendor to get out of the contract.

A *warranty* is a minor promise that does not go to the heart of the contract. If there is a breach of warranty, the purchaser cannot cancel but must complete the contract and sue for damages. Therefore, if a particular requirement on your part is pivotal to your decision to purchase the condominium or not, it is important to *frame your requirement as a condition rather than as a warranty.* Both vendors and purchasers frequently insert conditions into the agreement. These conditions are also referred to as *subject clauses* and should:

- Be precise and clearly detailed.
- Have specific time allocated for conditions that have to be removed, e.g., within two days to thirty days. It is preferable to put the precise date that a condition has be removed, rather than merely refer to the number of days involved.
- Have a clause that specifically says that the conditions are for the sole benefit of the vendor or purchaser, as the case may be, and that they can be waived at any time by the party requiring the condition. This is important, because you may wish to remove a condition even though it has not been fulfilled, in order for the contract to complete.

Here is just a sampling of some of the common subject clauses. There are many others possible that you or your lawyer may feel it appropriate to insert.

For Benefit of Purchaser

- Title being conveyed free and clear of any and all encumbrances or charges registered against the property on or before the closing date at the expense of the vendor, either from the proceeds of the sale or by solicitor's undertaking
- Inspection being satisfactory to purchaser by relative, spouse, partner, etc. (specify name)
- Inspection being satisfactory to purchaser by house inspector/contractor selected by purchaser
- Sale of purchaser's other property being made

- Receipt and satisfactory review by purchaser (and/or purchaser's lawyer) of project documents, such as disclosure, declaration, articles, rules and regulations, financial statements, project budget, management contract, estoppel certificate, etc.
- Confirmation of mortgage financing
- Approval of assumption of existing mortgage
- Vendor take-back mortgage or builder's mortgage
- Removal of existing tenancies (vacant possession) by completion date
- Confirmation by condominium corporation that the condominium unit being purchased will be able to be rented
- Existing tenancies conforming to prevailing municipal by-laws
- Interim occupancy payments being credited to purchase price
- No urea formaldehyde foam insulation (UFFI) having ever been installed in the unit
- Vendor's supplying a certificate of estoppel at the expense of the vendor within x days of acceptance of the offer
- Vendor's warranty that no work orders or deficiency notices are outstanding against the property, or if there are, that they will be complied with at the vendor's expense before closing

For Benefit of Vendor
- Removal of all subject clauses by purchaser within 72 hours upon notice in writing by vendor of a backup bona fide offer
- Confirmation of purchase of vendor-back mortgage through vendor's mortgage broker
- Satisfactory confirmation of creditworthiness of purchaser for vendor-back mortgage
- Issuance of building permit
- Builder receiving confirmation of construction financing
- Registration of a subdivision

(c) Risk and Insurance
It is important that the parties agree to exactly when risk is going to pass from the vendor to the purchaser. In some cases the agreement will state that the risk will pass at the time that there is a firm, binding, unconditional purchase and sale agreement. In other cases the contract states that the risk will pass on the completion date or the possession date. In any event, make sure that you have adequate insurance coverage taking effect as of and including the date that you assume the risk. The vendor should wait until after the risk date before terminating insurance.

(d) Fixtures and Chattels
This is an area of potential dispute between the purchaser and vendor, unless it is sufficiently clarified. A *fixture* is technically something permanently affixed to the property; therefore, when the property is conveyed

the fixtures are conveyed with it. A *chattel* is an object which is moveable; in other words, it is not permanently affixed. Common examples of chattels are clothes washer and dryer, refrigerator, stove, built-in microwave, and drapes.

A problem can arise when there is a question of whether an item is a fixture or a chattel. For example, an expensive chandelier hanging from the dining room ceiling, gold-plated bathroom fixtures or drapery racks, or television satellite dish on the roof might be questionable items. One of the key tests is whether the item was intended to be attached on a permanent basis to the property and therefore should be transferred with the property, or whether it was the intention of the vendor to remove these items and/or replace them with cheaper versions before closing the real estate transaction.

In general legal terms, if it is a fixture and it is not mentioned in the agreement, it is deemed to be included in the purchase price. On the other hand, if it is not a fixture and no reference is made to it in the agreement, then it would not be included in the purchase price. To eliminate conflict, most agreements for purchase and sale have standard clauses built into them which state that all existing fixtures are included in the purchase price except those listed specifically in the agreement. In addition, a clause should list the chattels specifically included in the purchase price, and they should be clearly described.

(e) Adjustment Date

This is the date that is used for calculating and adjusting such factors as taxes, maintenance fees, rentals, and other such matters. As of the adjustment date all expenses and benefits go to the purchaser. For example, if the maintenance fee has been paid for the month of March by the vendor and the purchaser takes over with an adjustment date as of the 15th of March, there will be an adjustment on the closing documents showing that the purchaser owes half of the amount of the prepaid maintenance fee to the vendor for the month of March. A discussion of adjustments for property tax is included the chapter on financing (Chapter 3).

(f) Completion Date

This is the date when all documentation is completed and filed in the appropriate registration and all monies are paid out. The normal custom is for all the closing funds to be paid to the purchaser's solicitor a few days prior to closing. As soon as all the documents have been filed in the land registry office and confirmation has been obtained that everything is in order, the purchaser's solicitor releases the funds to the vendor's solicitor. More discussion of the steps taken by both the solicitors relating to the closing date is presented later in this chapter.

Note: The adjustment date and the completion date are frequently the same.

(g) Possession Date

This is the date on which you are legally entitled to move into the premises. It is usually the same date as the adjustment and completion date. Sometimes the possession date is a day later in order for the vendor to be able to move out; in practical terms, though, many purchasers prefer the adjustment, completion, and possession dates to be the same, and make prior arrangements in terms of the logistics, if it can be arranged. One of the reasons is that the risks of the purchaser take effect as of the completion date, and there is always a risk that the vendor could cause damage or create other problems in the premises if he remains there beyond the completion date. As soon as your solicitor has advised you that all the documents have been filed and money has changed hands, the realtor or lawyer that you have been dealing with arranges for you to receive the keys to the premises.

(h) Merger

This is a legal principle to the effect that if the agreement for purchase and sale is to be "merged" into a deed or other document, the real contract between the parties is in the document filed with the land registry. To protect you, it should be stated in the agreement for purchase and sale that the "warranties, representations, promises, guarantees, and agreements shall survive the completion date." There are exceptions to the document of merger in cases of mistake or fraud, technical areas that require your lawyer's opinion; but it is important to understand the concept.

(i) Commissions

At the end of most purchase and sale agreements there is a section setting out the amount of the commission charged, which the vendor confirms when accepting an offer. Occasionally this section states that if the purchaser fails to complete the agreement after all "subjects" (subject clauses) have been removed, and therefore the sale collapses, the realtor can keep the deposit as a form of compensation. Naturally, if you are the vendor, you will not be pleased with this. You could therefore make sure the purchase and sale agreement states that if the sale collapses, at the option of the vendor the deposit monies can be deemed liquidated damages and the full amount go to the vendor. A discussion of the various types of agreements for listing and selling real estate through a realtor, the commissions, and how to select a realtor, is given at the end of this chapter.

C. OTHER LEGAL DOCUMENTATION

1. Project Documents

The *project documents* are registered with the land registry office (1) to create the condominium and (2) to deal with the administration or "government" of the condominium community. There is different terminology for these documents, depending upon the province: they are called a *description and declaration* in Ontario, Nova Scotia, New Brunswick, and Newfoundland; a *condominium plan and by-laws (schedule A)* in Saskatchewan and Alberta; a *strata plan and by-laws (first schedule)* in British Columbia; a *plan and declaration* in Manitoba, Yukon, and the Northwest Territories; and a *plan of the immoveables* and *declaration of co-ownership* in Quebec.

The project documents are executed by the owner/developer of the land on which the condominium is to be built. Although the contents of the project documents can vary from province to province, they all generally include the following:

- A plan or survey showing the perimeter of the horizontal surface of the land and the perimeter of the buildings
- Structural plans of the buildings
- A specification of the boundaries of each unit by reference to the buildings
- A diagram showing the shape and dimensions of each unit and the approximate location of each unit in relation to the other units and the buildings
- A certificate of a surveyor that the buildings have been constructed in accordance with the structural plans and that the diagrams of the units are substantially accurate
- A description of any interests relating to the land that are included in the property
- A statement of intention that the land and interests relating to the land are to be governed by the Condominium Act
- A statement of the consent of every person having a registered mortgage against the land and/or an interest relating to the land
- A statement of the proportions of the common interests, expressed in percentages
- A statement of the proportions in which the owners are to contribute to the common expenses, expressed in percentages allocated to each unit, and the proportions of the common elements to which each unit is entitled in the event of demolition or destruction

- A specification of any parts of the common elements that are to be used by the owners of one or more designated units and not by all the other owners (exclusive-use common elements)
- A description of the system of assessment for maintenance and operating expenses
- A statement of the fundamental rights and obligations of all parties involved
- A specification of common expenses
- A specification of duties of the corporation
- A specification of any allocation of the obligations to repair and to maintain the units and common elements

Obviously, the project documents are very important. In effect they are the constitution of each condominium corporation and are intended to be permanent in nature. In most provinces the project documents cannot be amended or changed in any fashion without the unanimous consent of the owners and mortgage holders.

2. By-laws

By-laws are created to assist the successful operation of the condominium project. They cover such matters as the use of common elements, the conduct of members of the condominium, and provisions for changes to the project and its rules. Basically, the by-laws are intended to provide a basis for the control, administration, management, enjoyment, and use of the individual units, common property, facilities, and assets.

By-laws can be amended or revised by a majority vote of the owners as outlined in the project documents. The term *by-laws* does not have the same meaning in every province. Some provinces set out in the condominium legislation the exact by-laws that have to be used; although these statutory by-laws can be amended by majority vote, any amendments have to be filed in the land registry office. Other provinces merely require in their condominium legislation that by-laws have to be established.

One example of a matter that could be contained in the by-laws is a limit on the number of residential condominium units that can be rented out by owners, the rationale being that tenants may not behave as responsibly as resident owners and that that could change the delicate mix of the condominium community. For example, there might be a provision that only 10% of the units may be rented out; if there are 50 units, that would mean a maximum of five units can be tenanted. Naturally this could be an important consideration to you. For example, if it was your intention to rent out the unit while you travel for two years, or if you intended to rent it out for investment purposes, you would need to thoroughly check into the by-laws and the number of units that are currently being rented out to see if the maximum has been reached. Alternatively, you may wish to look at another condominium development or, in the case of your travelling, have a condition in the offer to purchase that the offer is subject to consent from the condominium corporation to allow you to lease out the unit for a period of two years.

Other areas typically covered by the by-law provisions are:

- The number, qualification, nomination, election, term of office, and remuneration of the directors
- Matters relating to the meeting, quorum, and functions of the board of directors
- The appointment, remuneration, functions, duties, and removal of agents, officers, and employees of the corporation, and the security, if any, to be given by them to it
- The management of the property
- The use and management of the assets of the corporation
- The maintenance of the units and common elements
- Duties of the corporation
- Authorization of the borrowing of money to carry out the objects and duties of the corporation
- The assessment and collection of contributions toward the common expenses
- The conduct generally of the affairs of the corporation

3. Rules and Regulations

The legislation permits the condominium corporation to make such rules and regulations as it may consider necessary in relation to the enjoyment, safety, and cleanliness of the common property, common facilities, or other assets of the condominium corporation. The rules and regulations are intended to govern the everyday rights and obligations of the unit owners, and can vary according to the special needs and desires of each project. Check over the rules and regulations and make sure that you can live with them. Some of the more common rules and regulations are as follows:

- No barbecues are permitted on any patios without permission.
- No articles may be stored in the basement, except where stipulated.
- All common areas such as walkways, stairways, hallways, and entranceways must not be obstructed, in order to allow proper entry and exit from the building.
- Under no circumstances may children play in the public stairways, elevators, halls, or entranceways. Children are to play in the designated playground area only.
- No articles may be shaken or hung from any windows or patios.

- No wagons, bicycles, or similar vehicles may be stored in any of the public areas.
- Owners are not permitted to make any noises which could interfere with the rights and enjoyment of other owners.
- Dogs and cats are not permitted at all. Other pets must be confined strictly to the owner's unit, and these other pets cannot annoy or disturb neighbouring owners.
- Any complaints relating to the quality or nature of maintenance service is to be reported in writing to the management company.
- No owner is permitted to enclose a patio by means of a permanent structure, such as a solarium, without consent.

4. Disclosure Statement

Many provinces have a requirement that any sale of a new condominium by the builder/developer is not binding on the purchaser unless he has received a copy of a current disclosure statement. The Condominium Act which governs this requirement states that it only applies for residential purposes, and that if the disclosure statement is misleading or deceptive in any material sense, the party who has relied on the statement is entitled to damages for any loss suffered because of it. The types of provisions commonly contained in a disclosure statement are as follows:

- The name and municipal address of the person making the statement and the property affected by the statement
- A general description of the property or proposed property, including the types and number of buildings, units, recreational facilities, and other amenities, together with any conditions that apply to the provision of amenities
- The proportion of units, existing or proposed, which the declarant or proposed declarant intends to market in blocks to investors
- A brief narrative description of the significant features of the existing or proposed project documents, by-laws, and rules and regulations governing the use of common elements and units, and any contracts or releases that may be subject to termination or exploration pursuant to provincial legislation
- A budget statement for the one-year period immediately following the registration of the project documents
- If construction of amenities is not completed, a schedule of the proposed commencement and completion dates
- Any other matters that are required to be disclosed under provincial legislation

The budget statement referred to above should set out:

- The common expenses

- The proposed amount of each expense
- Particulars of the type, frequency, and level of the services to be provided
- The projected monthly common expense contribution for each type of unit
- A statement of the portion of the common expense to be paid into a reserve fund
- A statement of the assumed inflation factor
- A statement of any judgements against the corporation, the status of any pending lawsuits to which the corporation is a party, and the status of any pending lawsuits material to the property of which the person making the declaration has actual knowledge
- Any current or expected fees or charges to be paid by unit owners or any group of them for use of the common elements or part thereof and other facilities related to the property
- Any services not included in the budget that the person making the declaration provides or intends to provide, or any expenses he pays that might reasonably be expected later to become a common expense, and the projected common expense contributable to each of those services or expenses for each type of unit
- The amounts in all reserve funds
- Any other matters that are required to be disclosed under provincial legislation

5. Operating Budget

If you are purchasing a new condominium, in some provinces it is required that the developer provide budget projections and details as outlined in the preceding point. If you are purchasing a resale condominium, you should ask for the current or projected operating budget to review. (See Sample 1.)

6. Financial Statements

If you are purchasing a resale condominium, it is important to obtain copies of the most recent financial statements. Most financial statements are audited by a professionally qualified accountant and include the following: an accountant's comments, a statement of income and expenses, a balance sheet, and other documentation. Naturally, it is only as current as the most recent financial fiscal year-end, but it will give you a profile of the financial health of the condominium corporation. If you do not understand financial statements, you should have them reviewed for you by your lawyer or accountant, or on a consulting-fee basis by a condominium management company not involved with the project you are considering. For an example of a set of financial statements, refer to Sample 2.

7. Management Contract

This is an agreement between the corporation and the company that manages the project on a daily basis. The management contract can vary considerably from one development to another. The services provided include comprehensive ones such as operation, maintenance, and management. Under most provincial legislation, as soon as the majority of the units have been sold, the new buyers can cancel or modify the management agreement. This protects the public from a developer's signing a long-term management contract at an expensive price with an affiliated company before the units are put on the market. A more detailed discussion of management contracts was provided in Chapter 1.

8. Ground Lease

If you are purchasing a leasehold condominium, you will want to obtain a copy of the basic ground lease between the original landlord and the condominium corporation. This lease would set out all the terms and conditions of the relationship between the landlord (the lessor) and the tenant (the lessee).

9. New Home Warranty Program Certificate

The New Home Warranty Program is operated by the Housing and Urban Development Association of Canada (HUDAC). Most provinces have a New Home Warranty Program, although there are differences between the provinces in terms of coverages under the program. In some provinces the program is mandatory by law, whereas in others it is an optional program that builders may or may not be involved in.

It is important to contact the New Home Warranty Program in your province to get further information on the exact warranty coverage provided. Refer to Appendix A for a list of contact addresses in various provinces. The overall program applies to condominiums, apartments, townhouses, and other forms of residential homes, but in any particular province there could be some restrictions on the type of condominium structure covered.

Under the provisions of the Program, it is the builder's responsibility to repair, without charge, defects in materials and/or workmanship, and structural problems, according to the terms of the New Home Warranty Certificate. (As stated, the coverage can vary from province to province.)

In addition, any remainder of the warranty coverage applying to the previous owner is generally extended to subsequent buyers for a fixed period of time. Deposit funds are also protected up to a limit.

Prior to your taking possession of the condominium, under the Program you will be asked to inspect the building and note any deficiencies on a checklist form, and the builder will note on the form and if and when the problems will be remedied. Once you sign a certificate of completion and possession, this is filed with the Program and a New Home Warranty Program Certificate with an identification number is given to you. If a problem occurs after the signing, the homeowner notifies the builder; if the problem is not sufficiently addressed, the Program officials attempt to mediate the matter and rectify the problem within the limits of the coverage.

It is the builder who pays for the program, but sometimes the builder passes on the cost for each individual unit to the purchaser or otherwise adds it into the purchase price.

10. Estoppel Certificate

An estoppel certificate can be requested from the condominium corporation on application by the owner, the purchaser, or a purchaser's agent. It is deemed to be conclusive evidence of the accuracy of the facts outlined in it, and can be relied on by the purchaser. The following is an outline of the main facts confirmed by an estoppel certificate:

- The amount of the monthly maintenance charges paid by the owner that is applied to the condominium corporation's administrative expenses and contingency reserve fund
- The manner in which the monthly maintenance fees are paid
- The amount of money expended by the condominium corporation for the owner and not recovered by the owner
- The amount, if any, by which the expenses of the condominium corporation for the current fiscal year are expected to exceed the expenses budgeted for the fiscal year
- The amount of the contingency reserve fund
- That there are no amendments to the by-laws—or, if there are amendments, that those amendments have been filed
- That no notices have been given for a unanimous or special resolution that has not been voted on, other than those stated in the certificate
- That there are no proceedings pending against the corporation of which it is aware, other than those stated in the certificate

11. Insurance Trust Agreement

This is the document which provides for the distribution of insurance proceeds once a claim is made.

12. Statement of Recreational Amenities

This document outlines all the recreational and other facilities which are or will be provided to the condominium corporation. The document sets out details as to whether they will be owned or leased, and whether or not charges will be assessed for use by the members of the condominium corporation, and what those charges are or will be.

D. SELECTING A LAWYER

Whether you are the buyer or the seller of a condominium, it is essential that you obtain a lawyer to represent your interests—a normal precaution with any real estate transaction, but particularly important when dealing with a condominium. As you will realize by the time you have completed this book, there are many potential legal pitfalls for the unwary in the realm of condominiums. The agreement for purchase and sale and related documents are complex. To most people the purchase of a home is the largest investment of their life, and the agreement for purchase and sale is the most important legal contract they will ever sign.

When dealing with condominiums, it is important to select a lawyer who specializes in real estate law and is particularly familiar with condominium law. Laws are unique and constantly changing in this area, and expertise is therefore required. Because a lawyer who does a lot of condominium-related work has become familiar with the documentation, he or she will save you time and provide you with peace of mind.

There are a number of ways to select the right lawyer for your needs:

1. Ask friends who have purchased a condominium whom they used, whether they were satisfied with the lawyer, and why.

2. Contact the lawyer referral service in your community. Under this service, sponsored by the provincial law society or a provincial division of the Canadian Bar Association, you can consult with a lawyer for a half-hour for either a nominal fee (usually $10) or for free. Make sure you emphasize that you want a lawyer who specializes in real estate—ideally, condominium real estate.

Many provinces also have a "dial-a-law" service which provides free taped information over the phone on various legal topics relating to real estate and other issues. The duration of the taped message is generally seven to ten minutes, and it is normally available toll-free from anywhere in the province. Contact the law society in your province for further information.

3. Look in the Yellow Pages under "Lawyers" and check the box ads, which outline the areas of expertise.

4. If you are obtaining a mortgage, speak to the lawyer who is preparing the mortgage documents on behalf of the lender. If the lawyer you choose is also preparing the mortgage documents, you could save on some duplicated disbursement costs and negotiate a package price. Be cautious, though, to avoid conflict; you want to make certain that the lawyer provides you with a full explanation of the mortgage terms and conditions that might affect your interests. Keep in mind that the mortgage is being prepared on behalf of the bank, but at your expense. If you have any concerns in this area, obtain a separate lawyer to do the non-mortgage legal work.

Once you have made contact with the lawyer over the phone, enquire as to the areas of his or her real estate interest and expertise. Tell the lawyer that you are looking for a person with expertise in condominium law. If the lawyer cannot offer this, ask whom he or she would recommend.

If you did not obtain the referral through the community referral service, ask the lawyer over the phone what a half-hour initial consultation would cost. (In many cases it is free.)

Have all your questions and concerns prepared in writing so that you don't forget any. If you wish to make an offer to purchase, bring your offer-to-purchase document with you, and the details about the new or resale condo you are considering. Ask about anticipated fee and disbursement costs. If you are not pleased with the outcome of the interview for any reason, select another lawyer.

You may have heard the term "notary public" and assumed it means the same as "lawyers." This is not necessarily so.

In most provinces, a lawyer is also automatically a notary public, but a notary public is not necessarily a lawyer. Make sure you know the difference. A *notary public* is not formally trained, qualified, or permitted by law to provide a legal opinion on any subject. He or she can only prepare the required transfer of title documentation, necessary affidavit material, and other related documentary material, and file the documents in the land registry office. In other words, the services provided are primarily technical and procedural. Thus, the buyer or seller of a condominium is advised to consult a lawyer. In matters relating to condominiums, you certainly want a legal opinion considering the potential risk and pitfalls involved.

Note: In the province of Quebec, lawyers are referred to as "notaries" (non-courtroom lawyers) or "advocates" (courtroom lawyers). Therefore in Quebec you *would* use a "notary" for your condominium purchase or sale transaction.

In summary, make sure that you select a *lawyer*, and consult that lawyer before you commit yourself to any final agreement for purchase and sale.

E. SERVICES PROVIDED BY PURCHASER'S LAWYER

There are many services provided by your lawyer at various stages: before the agreement is signed, after the agreement is signed, just before closing the transaction, on the closing day, and after closing the transaction. What follows is a partial summary of some of the matters discussed and services performed in a typical real estate transaction. Each situation will vary according to the complexity and the nature of the transaction.

1. Before the Agreement Is Signed

* Discuss the contents of the offer to purchase with your lawyer. If there is a counteroffer by the vendor, make sure that you continue your communication with your lawyer before accepting the counteroffer, unless it is simply a matter of the purchase price.
* Discuss with your lawyer the ways in which you intend to finance your purchase.
* Enquire as to all the various legal fees and out-of-pocket disbursement costs that you will have to pay.
* Ask your lawyer about all the other costs related to purchasing the condominium that you should be aware of. The most common expenses are shown in Checklist 2.
* Discuss matters such as your choice of closing date, inspection of the property before closing, and any requirements that you want the seller to fulfill.

2. After the Agreement Is Signed

Once your lawyer has received a copy of the signed agreement, the process of thorough investigation is carried out, to make sure that all the terms of the contract are complied with and that you obtain clear title to the property without any problems. In other words, your lawyer will be going through a process of making sure that all your rights are protected and that you are getting what you contracted for. The types of areas that a lawyer will check include the items (a) to (n) that follow. *Note:* The first item is discussed at length.

(a) *Title of property:* An agreement for purchase and sale normally states that the vendor is going to provide title free and clear of all encumbrances. Therefore your lawyer has to make sure that there are no claims or other filings against the property that could impair the title that you are purchasing. When searching the title, you will be able to find out the name of the registered owner, the legal description, the list of charges registered against the property, and other documents that are filed against the property in the case of condominiums. The types of charges that may be shown against the property would include the following. (Different provincial jurisdictions may have varying terminology, but the concepts are the same.)

- Mortgage
- Right to purchase (agreement for sale)
- Restrictive covenant
- Builder's lien (claim for money owing)
- Easement
- Right of way
- Option to purchase
- Certificate under provincial family relations act restricting any dealing with the property
- Judgement
- Caveat (formal notice that someone has an interest in the property and the nature of that interest)
- Lis pendens (an action pending relating to the property—e.g., foreclosure proceedings)
- Lease or sub-lease, or option to lease
- Mineral rights by the government
- Condominium project documents
- Condominium by-laws

(b) *Survey certificate*

(c) *Property taxes*

(d) *Outstanding utility accounts*

(e) *Zoning by-laws*

(f) *Status of mortgages being assumed or discharged*

(g) *Ensuring financing will be sufficient and in place on closing*

(h) *Compliance with restrictions, warranties, conditions, and agreements*

(i) *Fixtures and chattels that are included in the purchase price*

(j) *Documents prepared by solicitor acting for seller (if applicable)*

(k) *Survey certificate*

(l) *All documents required relating to condominium purchase:* project documents, by-laws, rules and regulations, financial statements, disclosure statement, estoppel certificate, and other documents as required

(m) *Insurance obtained*

(n) *Mortgage reviewed*

3. Just Before Closing the Transaction

Just prior to closing there are various steps that your lawyer will go through, including:

- Preparing documents relating to any sales tax for the chattels that you may be purchasing.

- Signing any mortgage documents necessary and making arrangements for funding to the lawyer's trust account from the mortgage proceeds on filing
- Showing you a purchaser's statement of adjustments, which gives the balance outstanding that you have to come up with before closing the transaction. You normally have to provide these funds to your lawyer two days beforehand.
- Receiving for forwarding any postdated cheques required for the mortgage lender.
- Preparing all documents for filing in the land registry office on the closing date; if a different lawyer is involved in preparing the mortgage, that has to be coordinated for concurrent registration.

4. On the Closing Day

On the date of closing the transaction, your lawyer will perform various services, including:

- Checking on the search of title of the property to make sure that there are no last-minute claims or charges against the title.
- Releasing funds held in trust after receipt of mortgage proceeds from the lender if applicable, and sending an amount to the vendor's lawyer based on the amount they are entitled to as outlined in the purchaser's statement of adjustments.
- Receive a copy of the certificate of possession from the New Home Warranty Program, as applicable.
- Pay any monies required on the date of closing as outlined in the purchaser's statement of adjustments—e.g., sales tax on chattels being purchased, land transfer tax as applicable, and balance of commission owing to the real estate company, paid from the proceeds of the purchase funds due to the vendor—and as outlined in the purchaser's statement of adjustments.

5. After Closing the Transaction

Once the purchase has been completed, your lawyer will confirm that fact to you, and you can make arrangements with the realtor to obtain the keys to your home, or your lawyer will arrange to get the keys for you. Your lawyer will also:

- Send you a reporting letter with all the filed documents and all the other related documents attached for your records, including an account for fees and disbursements which have been taken from the funds that you provided your lawyer in trust prior to closing

- Arrange to obtain and register the appropriate discharges of mortgages that were paid off from the funds you paid for the purchase, unless the vendor's solicitor is attending to this obligation
- Ensure that all the vendor's promises have been satisfied

There are numerous costs involved in purchasing new property, as shown in Checklist 2. As to legal fees, you should be able to calculate accurately in advance, by making enquiries of your lawyer, the costs that you will have to budget for. Most lawyers charge a fee based on a percentage of the purchase price. In the case of condominiums, there is a higher charge generally, because of the extra documentation and responsibility involved on the lawyer's part, due to the nature of a condominium transaction. Although fees can vary from place to place because of market competition and other factors, between 3/4 and 1% of the purchase price is normal. (This relates only to legal fees and not to disbursements, which can vary considerably according to the nature of your transaction.)

F. SERVICES PROVIDED BY VENDOR'S LAWYER

If you are a vendor, it is important that you obtain a lawyer to represent your interests in the sale transaction. Whereas it is customary for the purchaser's lawyer to be paid a percentage of the purchase price, it is customary for the vendor's lawyer to be paid on an hourly basis for time actually expended. In view of the fact that condominium transactions are more complicated and therefore take longer, you can expect that they will be slightly more expensive than house purchases. The hourly bill-out rate would normally be between $75 and $150 or more, depending on the regional location and the lawyer's experience and expertise.

The lawyer acting for the vendor will perform a wide range of services, the extent of which depends on each transaction. Some of the services that will be performed at various stages are discussed below.

1. Before the Agreement Is Signed

Before you sign the agreement, you should have selected a lawyer whom you want to represent you, and discussed the contract with him to make sure that you are protecting your interests and not incurring any additional expense or unnecessary frustration. If you are presented with a written offer, there are basically three options open to you:

- You can accept the offer in the form in which it is presented, by signing the offer. In this event there is a binding contract between you and the purchaser.

- You can alter the offer, by making changes that are more suitable to you and having the offer resubmitted to the purchaser. By making changes to the purchaser's offer, you are in effect rejecting the offer and countering with a new offer. The purchaser can either accept your changes or make further changes and return the agreement to you, which constitutes a new offer.
- You can ignore the offer completely, if you feel that it is unrealistic or otherwise unsatisfactory to you.

2. After the Agreement Is Signed

Once the bargain has been reached in writing between the vendor and the purchaser, the vendor's lawyer will request various documents from the vendor in order to assist in completing the transaction. The type of material that you should obtain depends on the custom in your area and provincial jurisdiction. All the documents may not be easily obtained, but you should attempt to provide the following:

- Real estate tax bills
- Hydro or other utility bills
- Copies of insurance policies
- A survey, if you have one available
- A copy of the deed to your home, if you are in a province which has such a system
- A copy of any outstanding mortgages, with the address of the mortgage company, and if possible the mortgage account number and amortization schedule
- If an existing tenancy is being assigned, details on the tenancy and on any security deposits
- Any condominium-related documents, such as project documents, by-laws, rules and regulations, estoppel certificate, and others that may be required

Prior to completion of the transaction, you should make arrangements to notify the cable television and telephone companies that you want service disconnected from your address as of a certain date. Also, advise your insurance company to cancel the insurance policy on the day *after* the closing date.

3. Just Before Closing the Transaction

Your lawyer will prepare a deed or transfer document which you must sign before title can be passed to the purchaser. Your lawyer will also prepare the vendor's and the purchaser's statement of adjustments. In some provinces or regions, the custom is for the purchaser's lawyer to prepare the conveyancing (property transfer) documents for the vendor to sign and prepare the vendor's and the purchaser's statement of adjustments. These would then be forwarded for review to the vendor's solicitor and to the vendor before signing.

If a mortgage exists on your home, it is the responsibility of the vendor to discharge the mortgage in order that clear title to the property can be transferred. Your lawyer would obtain a copy of the mortgage statement showing the balance outstanding as of the closing date, and then "undertake" (legally promise) to the purchaser's lawyer that the mortgage would be paid off first from the proceeds of the purchase.

If you are a non-resident of Canada, there is a *withholding tax* that is to be kept back from the sale proceeds and remitted to Revenue Canada. This is because a non-resident could be making a profit or capital gain on the sale of the property, and is required to pay tax on that property; but Revenue Canada could have difficulty collecting from someone outside of the country. That problem is eliminated by having funds paid directly from the sale proceeds. How much should be held back varies with the circumstances. Your lawyer will advise you or find out the amount of the withholding tax.

4. On the Closing Day

On the date of closing, your lawyer or his agent will meet the purchaser's lawyer or his agent at the land registry office in order that the transfer documents can be filed, changing title.

5. After Closing the Transaction

After the transaction has been completed, and your lawyer has received the appropriate money based on the vendor's statement of adjustments, he will clear off any existing mortgages with those funds and have the mortgages discharged from the title of the property. You would then receive the balance of funds after the legal fees and disbursements have been deducted.

Finally, your lawyer will send you a reporting letter setting out the services that were performed and enclose any appropriate documents for your files.

G. SELECTING A REALTOR

There are distinct advantages to having a realtor acting for you in buying or selling a condominium. As in any profession, there is a range of competence among the over 80,000 licensed real estate sales people throughout Canada, but with careful selection you can minimize the risk and benefit greatly from the skills of a knowledgeable and sincere realtor.

1. How to Select a Realtor

There are a number of approaches to finding a good real estate agent:

- Friends, neighbours and relatives can be asked for the names of agents they have dealt with, and why they would recommend them.
- Open houses provide an opportunity to meet realtors.
- Newspaper ads list the names and phone numbers of agents who are active in your area.
- "For sale" signs provide agent's name and phone number.
- Real estate firms in your area can be contacted; speak to an agent who specializes in condominiums and is an experienced sales person.

After you have met several agents who could potentially meet your needs, there are a number of guidelines to assist you with your selection:

- Favour an agent familiar with the neighbourhood you are interested in. Such an agent will be on top of the available listings, will know comparable market prices, and can target the types of property that meet your needs as you have explained them.
- Favour an agent who is particularly familiar with the buying and selling of condominiums.
- Favour an agent who is experienced and knowledgeable in the real estate industry.
- Look for an agent who is prepared to pre-screen condos so that you are informed only of those that conform to your guidelines for viewing purposes.
- Look for an agent who is familiar with the various conventional and creative methods of financing, including the effective use of mortgage brokers.
- Look for an agent to be thorough on properties you are keen on, in terms of background information such as length of time on the market, reason for sale, and price comparisons among similar condominiums.
- Look for an agent who will be candid with you in suggesting a real estate offer price and explain the reasons for the recommendation.
- Look for an agent who has effective negotiating skills to ensure that your wishes are presented as clearly and persuasively as possible.

Because of the time expenditure by the agent, you should give the agent your exclusive business if you have confidence in him or her. Keep the agent informed of any open houses that you are interested in. Advise any other agents that you have one working for you. The reasons for these cautions will be explained in the next section, "The Listing Agreement." Focus clearly on your needs and provide the agent with a written outline of your specific criteria to assist in shortlisting potential prospects. If for any reason you are dissatisfied with the agent who is assisting you, find another agent as quickly as possible.

2. Benefits to the Purchaser

There are obvious benefits to the buyer of using a realtor as outlined in the previous points. One of the key benefits is that the realtor can act as an intermediary between you and the listing broker. That way, the listing broker never has an opportunity to meet you and therefore cannot exert any undue influence on you with aggressive salesmanship, or otherwise make an assessment of you that could compromise your negotiating position. The agent who has the listing agreement with the vendor would only know you through discussions with the realtor you are dealing with and through any offer that you might present. This "arm's length" negotiating position is an important strategic tactic that will benefit you.

Another advantage to a buyer is the opportunity for the realtor to access a multiple listing system computer, which can provide instant, thorough, and accurate information on properties that might interest you. Without an agent searching for you, you seriously minimize your range of selection and the prospect of concluding the deal at a price which is attractive to you.

3. Benefits to the Vendor

There are extensive benefits to listing your condominium with a realtor rather than attempting to sell it on your own. Some of the key benefits include the following:

- Realtors can list your property on the multiple listing service, which provides extensive exposure throughout and beyond your market area.
- Realtors can attempt to pre-qualify and pre-screen potential home buyers in order that only serious buyers who have the interest and financial resources present an offer.
- Realtors can provide information to the purchaser on matters such as financing and other assistance programs that could facilitate the sale of your property.
- Realtors can suggest methods of improving the appearance of your property in order to maximize the positive impression and therefore the potential buyer interest and sale price.
- Realtors can explain the real estate market in your area, and in a graphic fashion by providing you with computer printouts; and they can supply other facts and figures to assist you in realistically establishing a market price.
- Realtors free up your own time, using all their contacts and marketing techniques in order to effect the sale of your property.

- As is the case for purchasers, realtors negotiate an agreement on your behalf and according to your instructions, and you remain at arm's length from the one-on-one negotiating. This improves your negotiating position.

H. THE LISTING AGREEMENT

The real estate listing agreement is usually a partially preprinted form with standard clauses and wording. The balance of the agreement is completed by the agent and the vendor, and covers the specific information with respect to the property being offered for sale and the nature of the contractual bargain between the agent and vendor. Because the listing agreement is a binding legal contract, you should be very cautious about signing it without fully understanding the implications of what you are signing or obtaining advice from your lawyer beforehand. The following section covers the general contents of, and the types of, listing agreements.

1. Contents of a Listing Agreement

A listing agreement performs two main functions. You are giving the real estate agent the authority to act on your behalf to find a purchaser for your property. The agreement sets out the terms and conditions of this agency relationship, including the commission rate or method of compensation for the agent's services, the length of time of the appointment, when and how the fee or commission is earned, and how and when it will be paid to the agent.

Another feature of the listing agreement is the setting-out of the details of the property being offered for sale. All pertinent details should be set out, including civic and legal address, list price, size of condominium, description of the type of condominium (e.g, apartment or townhouse), number and size of rooms, number of bedrooms, type of heating system, main recreational features, and other amenities of the development. Any chattels or extra features that are to be included in the list price should also be set out—such things as appliances, draperies and drapery track, and carpeting.

You should also insert other particulars in the listing agreement relating to the property for sale, including details of existing financing, the balance on the mortgage, the amount of monthly payments, and the due date on the mortgage. Any other mortgages should be listed as well. Annual property taxes should be set out, as well as any liens, rights of way, easements, or other charges on the property.

Once you have come to an agreement on all the terms and you are satisfied with them, the agreement is signed and witnessed and you receive a copy.

2. Types of Listing Agreements

There are three basic types of agreements that you may wish to consider when listing your property with a real estate agent: open, exclusive, and multiple listing.

(a) Open Listing

In an open listing, the real estate agent does not have an exclusive right to find a purchaser for the property; you can sign any number of open listing agreements with as many different agents as you wish. Only the agent who sells the property earns a commission. But the problem with an open listing is that many realtors don't spend a great deal of time on the listing, because of the lack of assurance that they will ever receive a commission on the sale of the property. This is because so many other realtors could also be looking for purchasers.

Open listings are more common in commercial sales than in residential sales, and in any event you should obtain legal advice on the drafting of an open listing agreement if you are considering such an option. To protect yourself, make sure that the agreement is in writing and the terms clearly spelled out.

(b) Exclusive Listing

In this example, the vendor gives to the real estate agent an exclusive right to find a purchaser for the property. This right is given for a fixed period of time. The real estate agent is automatically entitled to receive a commission whether someone else sells the property, the vendor sells the property, or the property is sold at some future point to someone who was introduced to the property by the real estate agent during the listing period. An exclusive listing is normally for 30, 60, or 90 days. In many ways, the shorter the time period, the more energetically the realtor will have to work, and the more options you will have to change your realtor if you are dissatisfied with the performance and service.

(c) Multiple Listing

With a multiple listing, a realtor is given an exclusive listing, in effect, for a fixed period of time, but also the right to list the property with the multiple listing system (MLS). This system is computerized and is distributed to all members of the real estate boards who participate in the MLS. In practical terms, this constitutes almost all real estate companies;

the entire real estate network becomes like a group of sub-agents for the sale of your property. If some other agent finds a buyer, the selling company and the listing company split the commission equally. Multiple listings are generally for a minimum of 60 days.

CHAPTER

3

Financing

INTRODUCTION

Unless you already have sufficient cash to pay for a home in full, you will probably need to search for financing. This chapter covers many issues you need to consider. It will help you to understand the jargon and concepts to assist your selection process.

The chapter discusses such matters as financial needs assessment, types and sources of mortgages, how to calculate the amount of your mortgage eligibility, applying for a mortgage, costs of a mortgage, and mortgage default.

A. ASSESSING YOUR FINANCIAL NEEDS

If you have been considering the purchase of a home or condominium for some time, you probably have some savings already set aside for a down payment. You may be able to cash in your registered retirement saving plans (RRSPs), or borrow money from relatives. Possibly you already own a house and intend to sell it and apply the funds to purchase a condominium. You may already have a fairly clear idea as to the type of condominium that you are looking for.

In order to be realistic in your search, it is important to know the amount of mortgage that you are eligible for. This information, along with the knowledge of the amount of money that you can raise personally, will provide you with a price range for your new home.

Complete Sample 3, which outlines your personal financial needs. In addition, there are costs of closing on a home purchase and ongoing costs. The types of additional costs and expenses were covered in Chapter 2, and those specifically related to mortgages will be discussed later in this chapter. Refer to Checklist 2 for a detailed list of condominium purchase expenses you will have to consider.

B. WHAT IS A MORTGAGE?

A *mortgage* is a contract between one party who wants to borrow money and another party who wants to lend money. The borrower is referred to as the *mortgagor*, and the lender is referred to as the *mortgagee*. These terms can sometimes be confusing. The terms borrower and lender are also used. The mortgage agreement states that in exchange for the money which the lender is providing, the borrower will provide security to the lender in the form of a mortgage document to be filed against the property. For the purposes of this book, the term *property* will refer to the actual unit (whether a townhouse, a condominium, an apartment, or a detached unit) and the portion of ownership in the common property. The mortgage document specifies the rights that the lender has to the property in the event of default on the terms of the mortgage by the borrower. The types of remedies which the mortgagee has against the mortgagor will be covered later in this chapter.

A mortgage document filed against the title of the property in the appropriate provincial land registry provides security to the mortgagee against other creditors which the mortgagor may have. If a *first mortgage* is filed against the property and the mortgagee checks to make sure that there are no other encumbrances or charges against the property (types of encumbrances are discussed in detail in Chapter 2), then the amount outstanding on the first mortgage takes priority over any and all other creditors, i.e., it is paid off first from the sale of the property on default. Additional loans could be obtained by the mortgagor in which additional mortgages are filed against the property; a *second* or *third* or *fourth* mortgage could be filed against the property. Each mortgage ranks lower in priority than the previous, as the date of registration is the criterion that determines priority. Because of the increasing risk involved for subsequent mortgages, higher interest rates are charged. For example, the first mortgage interest rate may be 10%; the second, 12%; the third, 15%; and the fourth, 20%. The first mortgage would be paid out in full from any proceeds of sale, followed by the second mortgage and so on. It is possible that the price a home would sell for may only cover the payout on the first and second mortgages in this example, leaving no funds available to pay out the third and fourth.

Mortgages are regulated by federal and provincial law. Although the laws may be different from one province to another, the description of a mortgage outlined in this book applies to most mortgages. The method of mortgage registration and the enforcement laws are the main areas of variation between provinces. Some of the common clauses in a mortgage are discussed later in this chapter.

The difference between the amount that the condominium could be sold for and what you still owe on your mortgages is referred to as your *equity*.

C. TYPES OF MORTGAGES

There are several varieties of mortgages available from banks, credit unions, trust companies, mortgage companies, private lenders, government, and the vendor. Although most homeowners obtain financing through a conventional mortgage, it is helpful to be aware of other alternatives. The following is a brief discussion of the main types of mortgages.

1. Conventional Mortgage

The conventional mortgage is the most common type of financing for residential property. It is fairly standard in its terms and conditions, although there can be variations. In this type of mortgage, the loan cannot exceed 75% of the appraised value or purchase price of the property, whichever is the lesser of the two. This requirement is governed by law. The purchaser is responsible for raising the other 25% of the funds necessary, either through a down payment or through other means such as a second mortgage or vendor-back mortgage. Conventional mortgages are available through most financial institutions, including banks, trust companies, and credit unions. In most cases these mortgages do not have to be insured, but occasionally a lender may require it. For example, if the property is older or is smaller than is normally required by the policy of the lender, or if it is located in a rural or a run-down area, then the mortgage may be required to be insured with the Canada Mortgage and Housing Corporation (CMHC) or the Mortgage Insurance Company of Canada (MICC). CMHC is a federal Crown corporation, and MICC is the largest private insurer in Canada.

2. High-Ratio/Insured Mortgage

If you are unable to raise the necessary 25% funding to complete the purchase of the home, then a high-ratio mortgage may be available to you. These are conventional mortgages which exceed the 75% referred to earlier. By law these mortgages must be insured, and they are available only through approved lenders that are accepted by CMHC or MICC. Both these organizations have specific guidelines for qualifying, but the administration is done through the bank or trust company.

With MICC, the lenders have a fair degree of flexibility with regard to following their own policies and procedures. With CMHC, the lender must follow the special requirements laid down by the government. MICC can sometimes be more flexible in its policy with regard to the Gross Debt Service (GDS) Ratio permitted.

High-ratio mortgages are available up to 90% of the purchase price or of the appraisal, whichever is lower, and in some cases 95%. The percentage that you would be eligible for depends on various circumstances. There are also restrictions on the purchase price of the home that may be involved. Obtain further information from your realtor, banker, or mortgage broker, or MICC or CMHC directly. Contact addresses for MICC or CMHC are given in Appendix A.

3. Collateral Mortgage

In a collateral mortgage the mortgage security is secondary, or collateral, to some other main form of security taken by the lender. This main security may take the form of a promissory note, personal guarantee, or assignment of some other form of security that the lender may require. A collateral mortgage is therefore a backup protection of the loan which is filed against the property. The payment requirements on the loan are covered in the promissory note, and once the promissory note has been paid off in full, the collateral mortgage will automatically be paid off. You would then be entitled to have the collateral mortgage discharged from the title of the property.

One of the main differences between a collateral mortgage and a conventional mortgage is that a conventional mortgage can be assumed, whereas a collateral mortgage, of course, cannot be, as it is subject to some other form of security between the parties. Otherwise, the terms of the collateral mortgage could be very similar to the debt of a conventional mortgage. The money borrowed on a collateral mortgage could be used for the purchase of the property itself, or for other purposes such as home improvements, a business investment, or a vacation.

4. Government-Assisted Mortgage

National Housing Act (NHA) mortgages are loans granted under the provisions of this federal act. They are administered through CMHC. You can apply for a NHA loan at any chartered bank, trust company, or credit union. Borrowers must pay an application fee to CMHC which usually includes the cost of a property appraisal and an insurance fee. The latter is usually added to the principal amount of the mortgage, though it may be paid at the time of closing. Contact CMHC or your financial institution for the most current information on borrowing requirements.

In addition, some provinces have second mortgage funding available for home purchases. Generally there is a limit on the amount of the purchase price of the home, and a ceiling on the amount of the mortgage, usually $10,000. Obtain further information from your realtor or lending institution.

5. Secondary Financing

Secondary financing generally consists of a second mortgage and possibly a third mortgage. One of the reasons why you may wish to take out a second mortgage is because the existing first mortgage you are assuming has an attractive interest rate or has other desirable features, and because there will be a shortfall between the amount of your available down payment and the amount of the first mortgage. You therefore need to obtain funds. Chartered banks will usually provide money for second mortgages up to a limit of 75% of the lower of the purchase price and the appraised value. You can also obtain second mortgages through mortgage brokers or other sources that could go up as high as 90% of the lower of the purchase price or appraised value. If the second mortgage has a term that is longer than that of the first mortgage you assume, make sure that you have a *postponement clause* put into the second mortgage. With this clause you would be able to automatically renew or replace the first mortgage when it becomes due without having to obtain the permission from the second mortgage lender to do so. In other words, if you renewed the mortgage or obtained a replacement first mortgage, that mortgage would still be in first position, ahead of the second mortgage.

6. Assumed Mortgage

In the case of an assumed mortgage, you are qualified by the lender to assume an existing mortgage on the property. In some instances mortgages can be assumed without qualifications. If you assume the existing mortgage, it will save you the cost of legal fees and disbursements for registering the mortgage, obtaining appraisal, and other expenses. Whenever you are assuming an existing mortgage, it is important that your lawyer obtain for you a mortgage assumption statement showing the principal balance outstanding, the method of paying taxes, the remaining term on the mortgage and a copy of the mortgage which shows other features such as prepayment privileges, etc.

If you are a seller of the property, you should be very cautious about someone assuming your mortgage unless you obtain a release in writing from the lender that you will not be liable under the mortgage in the event that the person assuming it defaults on his or her obligations. In the event of default, the lender would be entitled to go after the original mortgagor as well as the person who assumed the mortgage, for the full amount of the debt outstanding or any shortfall after foreclosure proceedings and sale of the property has taken place. Make sure that you obtain legal advice before permitting any buyer to assume your mortgage.

7. Builder's Mortgage

If purchasing a new condominium, you may have the possibility of assuming the builder's mortgage. Make sure that you obtain legal advice before signing any such mortgage to ensure that the provisions in the mortgage are acceptable to you.

Another possibility is that the builder will offer you a discounted mortgage. In other words, to make the house price attractive, the mortgage rate might be reduced to 10%, whereas the prevailing interest rate for a first mortgage could be 14%. The builder is able to "buy down" a mortgage from a lender at an attractive rate by paying a discount—the difference in financial terms between what the lender would make on a 10% mortgage and what he would make on a 14% mortgage. However, builders frequently add on this discount to the purchase price of the home; you could be paying a lower interest rate because you are paying for a higher amount of mortgage than you normally would have to pay. You could also end up paying more interest over the term of the mortgage than you otherwise would have to pay. Another factor to be aware of is that the discounted mortgage may only be for a short time, e.g., a year, and after that period you will have to obtain your own mortgage at the prevailing rate. Thus, although a discounted mortgage could initially appear attractive, over the long term it could be false economy.

You may also be exposed to a "phantom mortgage." See the Glossary.

8. Vendor Mortgage

A vendor mortgage is sometimes referred to as a vendor-back or vendor take-back mortgage. Here, the vendor encourages the sale of the property by giving the purchaser a loan on the purchase of the property. For example, if the purchaser is able to get 75% conventional financing, but does not have sufficient funds for a down payment of 25%, the vendor may be prepared to give, in effect, a second mortgage for 15% of the purchase price. That way, the purchaser would only need to come up with a 10% down payment. The purchaser would then make mortgage payments to the vendor as if a normal commercial lender held the second mortgage. If you are the purchaser, it is fairly common for the vendor not to make any credit check or any other financial assessment of you. On the other hand, if you are the vendor, for obvious reasons you should make sure that there is a provision in the offer to purchase that you can do a thorough credit check of the purchaser before deciding on granting the second mortgage.

Sometimes the vendor makes arrangements through a mortgage broker for the second mortgage to be sold at a discount as soon as the transaction completes. This way, the vendor gets cash immediately, minus, of course, the cost required to discount the mortgage and the broker's fee. Generally the mortgage has to have a fixed and not a floating rate if it is to be sold, and the terms should be at least a year to be attractive to a purchaser of the mortgage. If the vendor intends to sell the vendor-back mortgage, there is normally a precondition in it that the purchaser will co-operate with any credit checks and will agree to the mortgage being assigned, and that acceptance of the offer to purchase is based on a commitment from a mortgage broker that there is a purchaser for the second mortgage as soon as the sale completes.

If you are considering providing a mortgage-back, again it is important to be cautious and obtain legal advice in advance. There is a risk that the purchaser will refuse to pay on the second mortgage if there appears to be any problem with the condition of the property after the sale. Naturally the vendor or the assignee of the vendor's second mortgage could commence foreclosure proceedings, but in practical terms it is possible that the purchaser could attempt to raise defences. To discuss in any detail these types of problems is outside the scope of this book; they are raised merely to alert the reader to the need for competent legal advice in these unique situations.

9. Blanket Mortgage

A blanket mortgage is a type of mortgage registered over two or more properties. The purpose behind the mortgage is to provide the lender with additional property as security. It is normally used where a borrower wants more money than the lender is prepared to provide on the basis of one property alone. That property may not have sufficient equity and, for example, the amount of money that is being requested could constitute 90% or 95% of the value of the first property. If the second property has attractive equity, the lender may be prepared to advance the funds to the borrower, but have one mortgage filed against both properties. In the event of default, the lender could proceed against one or both of the properties in order to get sufficient proceeds from sale to satisfy the outstanding debt.

Blanket mortgages are very common in condominium projects. The developer normally has a blanket mortgage over all the individual units and common areas. On the basis of this blanket mortgage, a lender will advance funds for the completion of the project. As soon as a unit is sold, the lender releases the portion of the blanket mortgage that was filed on the title of that unit in order for the purchaser of the unit to place his own mortgage. The developer normally has a requirement with its lender that all or a portion (for example, 50% or 75%) of the purchase price of the condominium unit has to be paid to the lender to reduce the blanket mortgage as a condition for the lender's releasing the encumbrance on that unit.

10. Leasehold Mortgage

A leasehold mortgage is a mortgage on a house or condominium where the land is rented rather than owned. The mortgage must be amortized over a period that is shorter than the length of the land lease. Normally a lender will not grant a mortgage on leasehold property unless the duration of the lease is of sufficient length that the risk is fairly minimal to the lender. For example, if a condominium is on leasehold land with a 99-year lease and there are 85 years left on the lease, then there is relatively little risk to the lender. On the other hand, if the leasehold is for a 30-year period and there are 5 years left on the lease, the lender will consider the risk too high, because at the end of the 5-year period the lease will expire and therefore there is no right or entitlement to the leasehold interest. This would mean that the condominium would have no value to a potential purchaser after 5 years.

11. Condominium Mortgage

In many cases condominium mortgages are identical to any of the other mortgages discussed in terms of the provisions, except for a few special provisions in view of the unique nature of a condominium. Although a purchaser of a condominium receives a legal title to one individual unit, the purchaser also has an undivided interest in the common elements of the development.

Some of the special clauses contained in most condominium mortgages that distinguish this type of mortgage from a conventional house mortgage are as follows:

- The lender has the right to use the unit owner's vote or consent in the condominium corporation. In other words, the lender has a proxy to vote in place of the borrower. In practical terms, the lender does not usually vote on any and all decisions in normal circumstances. The lender, though, does require that the borrower provide notice of all condominium corporation meetings, including special or extraordinary meetings announced by the condominium corporation, and copies of minutes and information.
- The lender requires that the borrower comply with all the terms of the by-laws, rules, and regulations of the condominium corporation. Any default on the borrower's part will constitute default under the mortgage.

- The lender requires the borrower to pay all costs of maintenance of the common elements. In the event of failure of the borrower to do so, the lender is entitled to pay the costs on behalf of the borrower and add these onto the principal amount outstanding on the mortgage, with interest charged to this amount.

12. Agreement for Sale

An agreement for sale is not actually a mortgage, but it is another way of financing a sale. It should not be confused with an agreement for purchase and sale. An agreement for sale is normally used in a situation wherein the buyer of the property does not have sufficient funds for down payment and the vendor wishes to dispose of the property. In an agreement for sale, the vendor finances the purchase of the property in a fashion similar to that of a vendor-back mortgage. The purchaser, though, does not become the legal owner of the property until the agreement for sale has been paid in full. At that time the purchaser is legally entitled to have the conveyance of the legal interest of the property transferred over to the purchaser. In the meantime, the vendor remains the registered owner on title of the property. The purchaser has the legal right of possession, and makes regular payments to the vendor under the terms of the agreement between the vendor and the purchaser. The purchaser has a legal "right to purchase" which is registered against the title of the property in the provincial land registry office.

The terms of an agreement for sale are in many ways very similar to the terms found in a mortgage. The agreement for sale may have a five-year term, for example, in which time the full amount is due and payable. At that time either the purchaser has to arrange conventional mortgage financing or other form of financing to pay off the vendor, or else make an agreement with the vendor for an extension of the agreement for sale for another term. Agreements for sale are frequently used where the purchaser cannot qualify to assume the existing mortgage or to obtain a new mortgage; in effect, the purchaser assumes a mortgage that would otherwise be unassumable.

D. SOURCES OF MORTGAGES

It is important to keep in mind that the competition for mortgage lending is extremely intense. There are numerous lenders of mortgage funds and they are all attempting to attract the customer to use their services. You should therefore do thorough research before deciding on which mortgage lender to use. Major city newspapers tend to publish a comparison of the prevailing mortgage rates by institution in the real estate section of the weekend newspaper. This will save you a lot of research time. Also check with mortgage brokers in your community. They frequently publish a list of current comparative rates and will send a copy to you free upon request. See the description of mortgage brokers in item (j) below.

The main sources of mortgage funds available for residential purchases that you may wish to consider are items (a) to (j) in the list that follows, some which are discussed at length.

(a) *Commercial banks*

(b) *Trust companies*

(c) *Credit unions*

(d) *Government:* As mentioned earlier, the federal government, through CMHC, provides mortgage funds if you qualify. In addition, many provincial governments have second mortgage funding available, again if you qualify.

(e) *A vendor-back mortgage*

(f) *Assumption of an existing mortgage*

(g) *Obtaining of funds from personal sources such as family, relatives, friends, or business associates*

(h) *Mortgage companies:* Check in the Yellow Pages under "Mortgages."

(i) *Real estate companies:* Many real estate companies that are owned by trust companies naturally have arrangements established for pre-approved mortgages. Because of the natural vested interest in terms of the connection between the real estate firm and the trust company, this can sometimes facilitate a more flexible gross debt service ceiling criterion in order for the sale to complete. Of course the usual financial qualification criteria for creditworthiness would apply.

(j) *Mortgage brokers:* Mortgage lending has become very complex, with constantly changing rates, terms, and conditions. Each lending institution has its own criteria that it applies to potential borrowers. Some insist on a particular type of property as security, while others require a certain quality or type of applicant. In this latter case, factors such as type of employment, job stability, income, and credit background are weighed. There is a broad range of philosophies and policies held by the various lending institutions on the issue of security and applicant qualifications in order for a lender to advance mortgage funds.

Other factors also impact on mortgage approval. Availability or shortage of funds, past experience in a specific area, perceived resale market for a particular property, and the attitude of the lending committee are all factors which could affect approving a mortgage.

Mortgage brokers make it their business to know all the various plans and lending policies and the lender's attitude on various aspects of mortgage security and covenants. A mortgage broker is in effect a matchmaker, attempting to introduce the appropriate lender to the purchaser.

Mortgage brokers have access to numerous sources of funds, including:

• Conventional lenders such as banks and trust companies

- CMHC
- Private pension funds
- Union pension funds
- Real estate syndication funds
- Foreign bank subsidiaries
- Insurance companies
- Private lenders

The broker knows all the lenders' objectives; the broker is therefore capable of matching the applicant and his or her property with the appropriate plan and lender. Alternatively, the broker can provide a series of mortgage plans from which the borrower may select the one that best suits his or her needs. The broker charges a commission fee, usually between 1 and 2% of the amount of the mortgage. In most cases the broker's fee is charged only if a suitable mortgage is found. Many mortgage brokers do not charge an advance fee from a client for processing a mortgage application. In some provinces there is legislation which prohibits a mortgage broker from charging an advance fee if the mortgage application amount is below a certain figure.

E. KEY FACTORS TO CONSIDER WHEN SELECTING A MORTGAGE

There are many factors you have to decide on before finalizing your mortgage decision. The key factors are amortization, term of the mortgage, open or closed mortgage, interest rate, payment schedules, prepayment privilege, and assumability. A brief explanation of each of these concepts follows.

1. Amortization

Amortization is the length of time over which the regular (usually monthly) payments have been calculated on the assumption that the mortgage will be fully paid over that period. The usual amortization period is 25 years, although there is a wide range of options available in five-, ten-, fifteen-, or twenty-year periods as well. Naturally, the shorter the amortization period, the more money you save on interest (see Chart 1).

2. Term of the Mortgage

The term of the mortgage is the length of time the mortgagee will lend you the money. Terms may vary from six months to ten years. If the amortization period was 25 years, that would mean that you have several different mortgages, possibly 10 to 20 separate terms before you have completely paid off the loan.

At the end of each term, the principal and unpaid interest of the mortgage become due and payable. Unless you are able to repay the entire mortgage at this time, you would normally either renew the mortgage with the same lender on the same terms, renegotiate the mortgage depending on the options available to you at that time, or refinance the mortgage through a different lending institution. If you renew with a different mortgage lender, there could be extra administrative charges involved. There being considerable competition among lenders, frequently there is no administrative fee if you are transferring a mortgage to another institution. In some cases another institution will absorb the legal fees and costs as well, as an inducement for you to bring the business away from a competitive lender.

Some people take out short-term mortgages (for example, for six months), anticipating that interest rates will go down and that at the end of six months there will be a lower interest rate. The problem is that if rates have gone up instead of down at the end of the six months, your monthly mortgage payment will increase and you may not be able to afford, or want to pay, the increased rates. The other option you have is to negotiate a long-term mortgage (for example, for five years) so that you can budget for the future over a five-year period with certainty about the interest rates. The lender is not obliged to renew the mortgage at the end of the term. If the lender decides to renew, an administration fee of $100 to $250 is often charged.

3. Open or Closed Mortgage

An *open* mortgage allows you to increase the payment of the amount of the principal at any time. You could pay off the mortgage in full at any time before the term is over without any penalty or extra charges. Because of this flexibility, open mortgages normally cost at least a percentage point more than standard closed mortgages.

A *closed* mortgage locks you in for the period of the term of the mortgage. There is a penalty fee for any advance payment. A straight closed mortgage will normally have a provision that if it is prepaid due to the property's being sold or the death of the borrower, either a three-month interest penalty or, in some cases, a higher amount than that will be applied; or the penalty will be waived entirely, if the new purchaser of the property takes out a new mortgage with the lending institution. Some closed mortgages have a prepayment feature.

4. Interest Rate

There are various ways to calculate the interest: the *fixed rate*, which means the interest rate remains fixed for the period of the term of the mortgage (for example, one year), and the *variable rate*, which means that the interest rate varies every month according to the premium interest rate set by the lender every month. In this latter case, although the actual monthly payments that you would make would usually stay the same, the interest charge proportion of that monthly payment of principal and interest will vary with that month's rate.

How often interest is *compounded*—in other words, the interest charged on interest owing—will determine the total amount of interest that you actually pay on your mortgage. Obviously, the more frequent the compounding of interest, the more interest you will pay. The lender can charge any rate of interest, within the law, and compound that at any frequency desired. That is why it is important for you to check on the nature of the compounding on interest.

By law, mortgages have to contain a statement showing the basis on which the rate of interest is calculated. Mortgage interest has traditionally been compounded on a half-yearly basis. If a mortgage is calculated on the basis of straight interest, that means there is no compounding, but just the running total of the interest outstanding at any point in time. Some mortgages, such as variable-rate mortgages, are compounded monthly. The rate quoted for a variable-rate mortgage is called a *nominal rate*, whereas the equivalent rate for "normal" mortgages (compounded semi-annually or annually) is called the *effective rate*. As an example, a mortgage which quotes a nominal rate of 10% has an effective rate of interest of 10% when compounded yearly, 10.25% when compounded half-yearly, and 10.47% when compounded monthly.

5. Payment Schedules

As to payment schedules, there are many options available in the marketplace, including weekly, biweekly (every two weeks), monthly, semi-annually, annually, and other variations. Naturally, the more frequently you make payments, the lower the amount of interest that you will be paying. (See Chart 2.)

Depending on your negotiations with the lender, you may make payments on interest only, or have a graduated payment schedule, which means that at the beginning of the term of the mortgage your payments are lower and increase over time so that at the end of the term the payments will be considerably higher. The reason for this type of arrangement is that the ability of the borrower to pay the payment will be able to increase over time, and the payment schedules are graduated to accommodate that.

Normally payments are made on the mortgage which are a blend of principal and interest. These have traditionally been amortized assuming a monthly payment basis.

6. Prepayment Privilege

This is a very important feature to have in your mortgage if your mortgage is a fixed mortgage. If it is an open mortgage, you can pay in part or in full the balance outstanding on the mortgage at any time without penalty. If on the other hand you have a closed mortgage which does not have any prepayment privileges, you are locked in for the term of the mortgage (for example, three years) without the privilege of prepaying without penalty.

You may therefore wish to have a mortgage which, though called a closed mortgage, is in fact partly open and partly closed, permitting prepayment at certain stages and in a certain manner, but not at other times. For example, you may be permitted to make a prepayment of between 10 and 15% annually on the principal amount outstanding. This could be made once a year at the end of each year of the mortgage. Another variation would also give you the option of increasing the amount of your monthly payment by 10 to 15% once a year. You can see the incredible difference this would make in terms of saving on interest and reducing the amortization period. Every time a prepayment is made, or every time you increase your monthly payments, the balance owing, and thus the monthly cost of interest, is reduced. For a graphic illustration, see Chart 3. The net effect is that a larger portion of each payment will be applied toward the principal, since monthly (or other agreed-upon regular) payments usually remain the same.

Make sure that you completely understand your prepayment options, as they could save you a lot of money. On the other hand, you may not want to have an open or partially open mortgage. If it appears that you are unlikely to sell your premises before the end of the term or to have any additional money to prepay the mortgage by using the prepayment features, it may be a prudent idea for you to consider a closed mortgage without any prepayment privileges because of the lower interest rate involved. It is important to make a realistic assessment of the right package for your needs.

7. Assumability

Assumability means that the buyer takes over the obligation and payments under the vendor's mortgage. Most mortgage contracts deal with the issue of assumability very clearly. The lender can agree to full assumability without qualifications, assumability with qualifications, or no assumability. For example, if a vendor reluctantly gave a vendor-back second mortgage for $50,000 for a period of two years, the vendor (the lender) may not want to have that mortgage assumed by anyone else, as the vendor would prefer to be paid out in full in the event that the property is sold, rather than carry the mortgage any longer.

The issue of assumability is an important one to consider. You would be able to have a wider range of potential purchasers interested in buying your home if purchasers who may not otherwise be able to qualify for your mortgage would be able to assume it without qualifications. Most mortgages though, have a clause that says that the mortgage is assumable with qualification by the lender.

F. GENERAL CONTENTS OF A MORTGAGE

Most mortgage documents are in fine print and are fairly detailed. There are no standard clauses in a mortgage. The only way you can fully understand your mortgage is to have a competent and experienced real estate lawyer review it and interpret the key areas for you. In addition to differences in mortgage contracts, the laws are in a constant state of change. Many people sign mortgages without having any idea what is in them. The purpose of this section is to outline some of the terms that you should be familiar with so that you will be better prepared when discussing the matter with a lawyer.

In any mortgage, there are these basic provisions: the date of the mortgage, the names of the parties who are signing, a legal description of the property, the amount of the loan, the payment terms including interest and frequency, the respective obligations of the lender and the borrower, and the signatures of all the parties. Some of the common clauses that you may find in the mortgage are discussed under headings 1 to 14 below.

1. Special Clauses relating to a Condominium Purchase

These have been covered under the section on types of mortgages.

2. Personal Guarantee

Under a mortgage, the borrower is personally liable for the debt to the lender. In the event of default, the lender can sue the borrower for the full amount of the mortgage; the lender is not obliged to commence foreclosure proceedings and take over the property or sell the property. In practical terms, however, the lender normally commences a form of foreclosure action to protect its interest as well as suing the borrower personally. If the property is sold, then the borrower would be responsible for the shortfall plus all the associated legal and other costs which the lender has incurred. If you have a *co-covenantor* on the mortgage—someone else who covenants or promises that he will meet all the obligations of the mortgage—the lender can sue both the borrower and the co-covenantor for the debt under the mortgage. (Sometimes the term *guar-*

antor is used instead of *co-covenantor*. In practical terms they are inter-changeable.) The lender may refuse to give funds covered by a mortgage without extra security protection by means of an additional guarantor or co-covenantor. If you are married and are purchasing the condominium under your personal name, the lender will almost always insist on your spouse's signing as a guarantor or co-covenantor, regardless of your creditworthiness. This is to protect the lender under the matrimonial or family relations legislation of the province: in the event that a separation or divorce occurs, the lender does not want its property security to be compromised.

3. Insurance

This clause requires that the mortgagor insure the condominium against fire. The insurance policy must show that the mortgagee is entitled to be paid first from the mortgage proceeds in the event of a claim on the policy.

There is also a provision in the mortgage which sets out the amount of the insurance (replacement). It states that if you fail to pay the premium, the mortgagee can do so, or if you fail to get sufficient insurance, the mortgagee can do so, and all the additional premium costs can be added onto the principal amount of debt of your mortgage.

4. Maintain Property

This clause in the mortgage states that you are required to keep the property in good repair. The reason for this provision is that the lender obviously does not want the property to deteriorate through neglect and therefore reduce its property value, compromising the value of the security.

5. Requirement to Pay Taxes

This clause states that you are obliged to pay all property taxes when they become due, and that if you do not do so, the lender is entitled to pay the taxes and add the amount paid in taxes to the principal amount of the mortgage. Many lenders attempt to avoid any problem with taxes by having a separate tax account set up at the time you take out the mortgage. This means that you pay an extra amount every month on your payment to the bank for a tax portion which goes into that account, and once a year the lender pays the property taxes directly. In many cases you can negotiate out of this prepayment provision and look after the taxes yourself. Some lenders require proof that taxes are current and have been paid every year.

6. Requirement to Keep Any Subsequent Mortgages in Good Standing

This provision states that you must maintain all your financial obligations on the second and third mortgages so that they do not go into default. If they do go into default, foreclosure proceedings could occur. If the property was sold, the first mortgage would be paid off first, followed by the second and the third.

7. Prohibition against Renting Out Premises

Some mortgage documents state very clearly that the premises cannot be rented out. This is fairly common with CMHC residential mortgages, as they are granted for the benefit of the owner/occupier and not for investment or rental purposes.

8. Must Comply with All Laws

This provision would advise that all federal, provincial, and municipal laws concerning the use and occupancy of the property must be fully complied with. This is an important provision if you are intending to rent out the property. Although there may not be a strict prohibition against rental, indirectly there could be if municipal zoning by-laws prohibit rental of residential premises.

9. No Urea Formaldehyde Foam Insulation (UFFI)

Many mortgages state that no UFFI is permitted in the premises at the time the mortgage is granted or subsequently.

10. Prepayment Privileges

It is important that you make sure the prepayment privileges are set out clearly in the agreement. The various types of prepayment privileges have been previously discussed.

11. Assumption of Mortgage Privileges

Assumption of mortgage privileges should be set out clearly in the mortgage document. This subject also has been discussed earlier.

12. Quiet Possession

This provision states that unless the mortgagor defaults, the mortgagee will not interfere in any way with the peaceful enjoyment of the property by the mortgagor. In practical terms this means that the mortgagee cannot enter the premises.

13. Acceleration Clause

This clause states that if the mortgagor defaults on any of the terms of the mortgage agreement, then at the option of the mortgagee the full amount outstanding on the principal of the mortgage plus interest is immediately due and payable.

14. Default

This section of the mortgage deals with the type of matters which could place the mortgagor in default of the mortgage agreement, and sets out the rights of the mortgagee in the event of default.

Refer to Checklist 3 when negotiating with a lender. Again, be certain that you have your lawyer advise you on the contents of the mortgage before signing it.

G. DETERMINING THE AMOUNT OF MORTGAGE AVAILABLE

Different lenders have different criteria for approving the amount of mortgage funds available. There is considerable flexibility with many lenders and it is important to compare or have a mortgage broker do so on your behalf in order to get the maximum amount of mortgage funds possible in your situation. Lenders use the Gross Debt Service Ratio and Total Debt Service Ratio as standard formulas for determining mortgage qualification. There are other forms of calculations that you may want to utilize that would be helpful to you in determining the data relating to mortgages.

In calculating matters of principal and interest relating to mortgages and other factors such as different pay periods, you may want to obtain an amortization table or mortgage interest booklet. You can purchase these from most bookstores or stationery stores. Chart 4 is a sample mortgage amortization schedule. Also refer to Chart 5 showing monthly mortgage payments.

1. Gross Debt Service Ratio (GDS Ratio)

The GDS Ratio is used to calculate the amount you can afford to spend for mortgage principal, P, and interest, I, payments. Some lenders also include property taxes, T, as part of this formula, and possibly heating costs, H, as well. All these expenses are added together. Under the GDS Ratio, payments generally should not exceed 30% of your income. There is flexibility in lending criteria, though, as some lenders will go up to 32% and in some cases 35% of your income and only include P and I rather than PIT or PITH. Refer to Sample 4 to calculate your own mortgage eligibility.

2. Total Debt Service Ratio (TDS Ratio)

Many people have monthly financial obligations other than mortgage and taxes, and lenders want to know these in order to determine ability to debt-service the mortgage. Using the TDS Ratio, the bank would want to know your fixed monthly debts such as credit card payments, car payments, other loans, and condominium maintenance fees. In general terms, no more than 40% of your gross family income can be used when calculating the amount you can afford to pay for principal, interest, and taxes plus your fixed monthly debts. The lender is naturally concerned about minimizing the risk that you will be unable to meet your financial obligations relating to the mortgage if the ratio is too high. Refer to Sample 5.

It is important for you to consider all your monthly obligations, some of which may not be taken into account by the lender, so that you get a good feel for your financial standing—for example, insurance and electricity costs. Complete your personal cost of living budget, Sample 3. This should give you some idea, net of tax, of what your monthly income is and what your monthly debt-servicing charges will be on the mortgage plus other expenses.

3. Other Forms of Calculations

Here are some other forms of calculations that could be useful for you.

(a) To calculate gross monthly income required if you know the amount of mortgage needed:

Step 1: Determine the amount of mortgage required.

Step 2: Determine the interest rate.

Step 3: Obtain monthly income factor from the income factor chart, Chart 6. Select the factor next to the interest rate shown.

Step 4: Multiply the mortgage amount by the factor and divide by $1,000 to arrive at the monthly income required to pay the mortgage principal and interest (PI).

Example

PI	$100,000
Interest	11%
Monthly income factor	34
34 × $100,000 ÷ 1,000	$ 3,400
Monthly income required for PI	$ 3,400

(b) To calculate the maximum amount of mortgage available if you know your gross annual income:

Step 1: Normal maximum GDS Ratio is 32% of annual income. Gross annual income multiplied by GDS Ratio equals the maximum amount to service principal, interest, taxes, and heating (PITH), plus, if applicable, any secondary mortgage financing, ground rent (where land is leased and not purchased outright), and one-half of any condominium maintenance fees.

Step 2: Maximum amount to service PITH less annual taxes, annual heating cost, and, if applicable, the annual amount for any secondary mortgage financing, ground rent, and one-half of any condominium maintenance fees, equals the amount available to service principal and interest.

Step 3: The annual amount available for principal and interest is divided by the number of regular payments to be made over the year based on the frequency of payment chosen, to arrive at the amount available for each payment. (Monthly, 12 payments; semimonthly, 24; biweekly, 26; weekly, 52.)

Step 4: Divide this amount by the appropriate payment factor (see payment factor chart, Chart 7), and multiply by $1,000 to arrive at the qualified maximum mortgage amount.

Example

Gross annual income	$50,000
Annual taxes	$ 1,300
Annual heating cost	$ 900
Half of condominium fees ($200/month × 12 ÷ 2)	$ 1,200
Secondary mortgage financing	N/A
Interest rate	11%
Amortization period	25 years

Step 1
$50,000 × 32% (GDS Ratio) $16,000

Step 2

Subtract: Taxes	(1,300)
Subtract: Heating cost	(900)
Subtract: Half of condominium fees	(1,200)
Annual income available to service mortgage (PI)	$12,600

Step 3
Assume payment frequency chosen is on a monthly basis. Therefore $12,600 ÷ 12 = $1,050 per month.

Step 4
Monthly payment factor at 11% interest rate is 9.62529.
$1,050 ÷ 9.62529 × $1,000 = $109,087
Maximum mortgage amount is thus $109,087.

(c) To calculate the maximum price for a condominium you can afford if you know the maximum mortgage available:

Step 1: Take the maximum mortgage available amount calculated in (b). Assume this represents a conventional mortgage up to 75% of purchase price.

Step 2: Add the savings and other sources of financing you have available representing 25% of the mortgage amount. If you are unable to raise the 25%, you would probably have to reduce the purchase price by the difference between the mortgage and what you can raise. Alternatively, you could apply for high-ratio financing and put down 10% of the purchase price, or attempt to obtain a higher GDS Ratio.

Example

Maximum mortgage amount available (representing 75% of
purchase price) $109,087.00
Maximum down payment available (25%) 27,271.75
Maximum house price $136,358.75

(d) To calculate gross annual income required if you know the amount of monthly mortgage payments for principal and interest (P + I), multiply the monthly mortgage payments for principal, interest, and taxes (PIT) by a factor of 40. This will give you an appropriate figure for gross annual income.

Example

Monthly payments for principal and interest .... $ 900
Monthly property taxes (T) (annual taxes ÷ 12) 100
Total PIT $1,000

Since $1,000 × 40 = $40,000, the gross annual income required is (approximately) $40,000.

Example

If the lender uses heating costs (H) when calculating your GDS Ratio, your salary to qualify for the same mortgage as above will have to be higher.

Monthly payments for PIT $1,000
Monthly heating costs (H) 100
Total PITH $1,100

Since $1,100 × 40 = $44,000, the gross annual income required is (approximately) $44,000.

H. APPLYING FOR A MORTGAGE

In applying for a mortgage, there are various steps you should follow to make sure you obtain the funds you need on the terms and conditions you want.

1. Preparation for the Application Interview

Here is a summary of the steps that you should follow prior to any interview:

(a) Complete your comparison shopping of all the types of lending institutions that you could obtain mortgages from. Check competing interest rates for different types of mortgages by contacting a mortgage broker to obtain a current schedule. Refer to your local newspaper to see if it regularly prints comparative mortgage rates.

(b) Understand the jargon. This book should help you to know what you want from a mortgage, and therefore negotiate the package that is suited to your purposes.

(c) Determine the questions that you want to ask the lender, using Checklist 3 as a guide, and think up additional questions that you may want to ask.

(d) Determine your financial needs. Complete the cost of living budget, Sample 3, as well as the mortgage checklist.

(e) Calculate the maximum amount of mortgage available that you might be able to expect from a lender. (Refer to the previous section, which provides the necessary formulas.)

(f) Obtain a letter of confirmation of employment from your employer, if you are employed. This would confirm your salary, your position, and the length of time you have been with that employer. If you are self-employed, you will be required to bring copies of recent financial statements or income tax returns.

(g) Prepare a statement of your assets and liabilities and net worth. Refer to Sample 6, the mortgage application form.

(h) Complete details on the amount of the down payment that you will be providing and where the funds are coming from. This last could include savings accounts, term deposits, Canada Savings Bonds, RRSPs, a family loan, an inheritance, a divorce settlement, proceeds from the sale of a house, or other sources.

(i) Complete the sample mortgage application form (Sample 6).

(j) Obtain a copy of the offer to purchase.

2. The Application Process

The steps to this process are as follows:

(a) You have to personally attend at the lending institution, generally along with your spouse and any co-applicant or guarantor.

(b) A formal mortgage application has to be completed. The application is typically divided into three main sections: description of the property, financial details relating to the purchase of the property, and personal financial information.

(c) Processing of the application by the lender normally takes between two and five business days. During that time the lender will:

- Check your credit references and your credit rating
- Verify the financial information you have given
- Have the property appraised (at your cost)

- Assess your application within the lender's approval guidelines
- Issue a formal commitment of approval in writing

(d) Different lenders have different guidelines when assessing mortgage applications, but generally there are three main criteria: Character, capacity, and collateral.

Character: The lender will be attempting to make an assessment of your credit history, and other factors as well, with a view to predicting how you will meet your obligations in the future. For example, do you regularly pay your bills on time? What is your credit rating in terms of your credit history in previous loans that you have had? Do you seem to be dependable in terms of the duration that you have been at your job? Or have you had a different job every three or four months?

Capacity: The lender is concerned about your ability to meet your financial obligation, and will be concerned about such questions as: Does your GDS Ratio come within their guidelines? What are your other debts and obligations? Is your income sufficient to handle the mortgage payments? Is your income stable, and does it appear as though it will continue to be so?

Collateral: Lenders are very much concerned with knowing that the security which has been provided for a loan is sufficient to cover the loan in the event that it is not repaid. That is why they use their own appraisers for assessing the value of a property; generally they want to have a conservative appraisal of the property as an extra caution. The lender wants to be satisfied that the property being offered as security could be readily sold if necessary. When making an appraisal and therefore determining the value of the security that is being pledged as collateral, the following factors are considered: location, price, zoning, condition of the housing unit, quality of neighbourhood, size, appearance, municipal services available, and comparative condominium sales in the same area.

3. Pre-approved Mortgage

You should be aware of the concept of a *pre-approved mortgage*. This is fairly popular with most conventional lending institutions and with trust companies and credit unions. The purpose is to give you a precise amount of money that you can rely on for mortgage purposes when you are out searching to buy a home and negotiating a purchase. You are given a fixed amount of mortgage for a period of time, for example, $100,000 with an interest rate that would be guaranteed for 90 days. There is always a condition, of course, that the lender must approve the actual property being purchased, before you can enact a final contractual offer to purchase. This provides the lender with an opportunity to make sure that the security is suitable.

4. Loan Approval

When the lender is in the process of approving the loan, the amount lent is an important consideration. As discussed earlier, if the amount is over 75% of the appraised value or the purchase price, whichever is lower, the mortgage has to be insured as a high-ratio one.

Once the lender has granted approval for the mortgage, the lender will appoint its own lawyer to protect its interests by checking on the title of the property to make sure that it is clear, and to perform any necessary duties, including the filing of the mortgage. Alternatively, the lender may allow the borrower's lawyer to perform the mortgage work. In either case the borrower customarily pays all the legal fees and disbursements. If you are required, or prefer, to use the lender's lawyer for preparing the mortgage documents, obtain independent legal advice about the provisions of the mortgage to make sure that the document sets out your intended bargain. Other legal aspects relating to the transfer of title of the property and the filing of a mortgage have been covered in Chapter 2.

I. COST OF OBTAINING A MORTGAGE

There are numerous direct and indirect expenses related to obtaining a mortgage. Not all the following expenses will be applicable in your case, but it is helpful to be aware of them. There are also additional expenses which are not covered in this chapter, as they really relate, not to obtaining a mortgage, but to purchasing a property and having the title of the property transferred over to your name. Expenses in this category include legal fees and disbursements, provincial land transfer filing fees, and property purchase tax, and were discussed in Chapter 2. Other potential expenses involved when purchasing a condominium include: new home warranty fee, condominium maintenance fee adjustment, utility connection charges, cost of repairs that may be required prior to occupancy, and moving expenses. (Refer to the condominium purchase expenses checklist, Checklist 2.)

Costs will vary considerably from one lender to another. The type of financing that you are obtaining will be a factor. The following sections discuss some of the most common expenses that you should consider and, if necessary, budget for.

1. Mortgage Application Fee

Some lenders charge a processing fee or set-up fee for their administrative expenses in the processing of your mortgage application. Avoid paying this type of fee if at all possible. Due to the highly competitive nature of the mortgage industry, many lenders do not charge any application fee for residential mortgage purposes. *Note:* If you are borrowing money for non-residential purposes, such as investing in property, this type of fee is fairly common because of the extra amount of work that is required in assessing the loan application.

2. Standby Fee

Some lenders attempt to charge a fee to the borrower for setting aside and reserving the money that the borrower requires until such time as the money is advanced. The rationale behind this fee is that the mortgage company will be losing revenue on this money on the interim. This is not a common fee for residential mortgage purposes and should be avoided. It is not, however, an uncommon fee for money borrowed for investment or commercial purposes.

3. Credit Investigation Report Fee

This is a fee that may be charged the borrower for the expense the lender incurs for doing credit investigation on the borrower. The fee may be either a separate fee or included in the mortgage application fee. Many institutions do not charge this fee and absorb it as a cost of doing business, as they hope to make money from you on the interest that you pay on your mortgage.

4. Appraisal Fee

The lender will obtain its own appraiser to determine the value of the security for mortgage purposes. The necessary fee is either paid by the borrower to the lender in advance at the time of application or is taken from the mortgage proceeds by the lender. In any event, the borrower pays the cost of the appraisal. Generally lenders will not give you a copy of the appraisal.

There is a possibility that you could save on the appraisal fee under certain circumstances. For example, if a vendor or purchaser has already arranged for a professional appraiser to evaluate the property, and the appraisal is not over 60 to 90 days old, the lender may be prepared to accept the appraisal if it approves of the appraiser, and if property values have remained the same or increased since the appraisal was made.

5. Survey Fee

If you are purchasing a new condominium, you will generally be required to obtain a property survey prior to mortgage funds being paid out. The survey would be done by a qualified professional surveyor, and the purpose is to make sure that the lender knows exactly the dimensions of the property that it is using as security. For example, a condominium may show as 1,200 square feet in size, but a survey could show that 900 square feet of that is liveable space and the other 300 square feet is a balcony— i.e., the balcony is considered part of your unit, and not as common or limited common elements. The lender may also want to be satisfied with the overall development to make sure that the building in which the condominium is situated meets the requirements for set-backs as required by the municipal by-laws. The cost of the survey would be deducted from the mortgage funds that have been advanced to you, or you would pay for it directly.

6. Mortgage Insurance Fees (CMHC or MICC)

If you are obtaining a high-ratio mortgage or the lender requires you to obtain mortgage insurance for other reasons, then you will be paying a mortgage insurance fee. The fee normally ranges between 1 and 2% of the amount of the mortgage that is being insured and is either added onto the mortgage total or paid by you in a lump sum at the time of closing the mortgage transaction. Mortgage insurance was discussed earlier under the topic of high-ratio mortgages.

7. Mortgage Broker Fee

If you use a mortgage broker to obtain financing, you will have to pay a fee, normally 1 to 2% of the amount of mortgage that was raised for you. This is paid at the time of closing. Most mortgage brokers would require an advance fee from you for appraisal costs and out-of-pocket costs that are incurred in advance. This is not the same as an application fee or administration fee, but could be included within such fees if they are charged.

8. Mortgage Life Insurance Premiums

Mortgage life insurance is not the same as mortgage insurance. Many of the lending institutions provide an option for you to purchase insurance that will pay off the mortgage in the event of your death, the premium for which is generally included in your monthly payments. You should compare with term insurance from private insurance carriers to see if the rates are competitive. As an option you may prefer to protect yourself by taking out your own term insurance which would be payable to your estate in the event of your death, your estate would then have sufficient proceeds to pay off the mortgage.

In certain circumstances a lender may require, as a condition of mortgage approval, that you take out the mortgage life insurance. This would normally only be in a situation where the lender felt your health to be a risk factor. Again, you could purchase your own term insurance or other type of life insurance and verify to the lender that you had such insurance. The lender may require that he be shown on the insurance policy as being paid first from the proceeds, but this would be an unusual type of request; it would be more likely if one were borrowing money through a mortgage for investment or commercial purposes.

9. Home Fire Insurance Premium

The lenders require that any borrower on a mortgage carry sufficient fire insurance to cover the amount of the mortgage, and that they be paid off first. The second mortgage lenders would want the same type of coverage and have it shown that they are paid off second, and so on. It is necessary for the borrower to purchase sufficient replacement insurance. The borrower is responsible for making insurance arrangements and paying the costs of the insurance premiums directly to the insurance company. A copy of the insurance policy showing the lender is on the policy as being paid first or second, as the case may be, has to be provided to the lender's lawyer before any mortgage funds are advanced.

10. Contribution to Property Tax Account

Many lenders require that you pay 1/12 of the projected annual taxes each month. This payment would be built into your monthly mortgage obligations, and the lender would set up a separate tax account and remit the taxes directly to the municipality at the appropriate time each year. Normally taxes are payable in June or July every year although they are calculated on the calendar year, that is, January 1st to December 31st. Some municipalities require an advance part-payment in February of each year and the balance in July of that year. If the lender makes the automatic monthly tax payment a condition of mortgage approval, make sure that you enquire as to whether interest is going to be paid on your tax account to your credit, and if so ask about the interest rate. The interest paid is normally lower than the interest paid on deposit accounts. The reason why some lenders require monthly payments is to minimize the risk that you will not have sufficient funds to pay the taxes every year; if this happened, the property could conceivably be put up for tax sale and jeopardize the lender's security.

In most cases lenders will give you the option to be responsible for paying your own taxes directly once a year. If you are paying a portion of the projected property tax every month, you will have to build that expense into the costs related to your mortgage.

11. Property Tax Adjustment Holdback

This concept is related to the previous topic. If the lender requires that you pay a portion of the property taxes every month, and if you purchase the condominium on April 1st with property taxes due in July, obviously there will be a shortfall in the tax account. In other words, if the property taxes are due and payable in full on July 1st, and you have made payments each month of 1/12 of the projected annual tax, then by July 1st the tax account set up by the lender will be short by 9/12 of the amount required to pay the taxes. The lender may require that you pay 9/12 of the projected annual tax into the tax account at the time of closing of the mortgage transaction. Either you would have to come up with these funds additionally or the lender would subtract that amount of money from the mortgage proceeds being made available to you. Alternatively you may be required to pay 4/12 of the projected property tax to the lender for each of the three months of April, May, and June prior to the tax payment deadline of July 1st.

12. Interest Adjustment

When you pay rent you are paying in advance. When you are paying mortgage payments to the lender for principal and interest, you are paying in arrears. In other words, if you make a mortgage payment on March 1st, it is to cover the use of the funds and the interest on those funds for the month of February.

Because the lender's internal system is geared on a monthly payment basis, assuming that it is a fixed interest rate, the lender will want to be paid in advance for the use of the funds from February 15th until March 1st. This interest adjustment is then advanced from the mortgage funds provided to you on February 15 so that the interest is prepaid up to March 1st. When your normal mortgage payment would be made on April 1st, it would cover the one-month interest for the month of March plus a small repayment of the principal. Not all lenders require this arrangement, but you should know in advance so that you are aware of the net proceeds that you will receive on the mortgage.

13. Interest

Interest is of course a cost of having the funds paid to you under a mortgage. What you will have to pay for interest, and the steps you should go through to obtain the most attractive interest rate, have been discussed.

14. Provincial Mortgage Filing Tax

Most provinces charge a tax or a fee for filing a mortgage in the land registry.

15. Legal Fees and Disbursements

You are responsible for paying the lawyer for legal fees as well as out-of-pocket disbursements that the lawyer incurs relating to the preparation and filing of the mortgage documentation. Disbursements would cover such things as property searches, photocopy expenses, courier costs, and other costs associated with the preparing and registration of the mortgage. The disbursement costs would normally include the provincial mortgage filing tax or fee referred to above. It is the normal practice for lawyers to deduct the legal fees and disbursements directly from the money to be advanced under the mortgage.

Sometimes lenders require that you use a particular law firm, or you have the choice of which one of several law firms you would prefer to deal with. Other times the lender will permit you to use a lawyer of your choice. In all cases you are responsible for the legal fees and disbursements.

J. DEFAULTING ON YOUR MORTGAGE

As long as you meet the payments and the terms as agreed with the mortgage company, the mortgage company cannot commence any action to foreclose on the property. On the other hand, if you have difficulty with your payments or breach any terms of the mortgage, there are very severe remedies that the lender has available to protect its security. Defaulting on a mortgage has potentially serious consequences. If you are consistently late, this could affect your credit rating, and also your ability to renew your mortgage or obtain other mortgages in the future.

This section will cover factors that constitute default, the mortgagor's options, and the mortgagee's options. (It is not within the scope of this book to go into any more detail on mortgage default or foreclosure than to give an overview of the issues to consider.)

1. Factors that Constitute Default under a Mortgage

The mortgage agreement sets out in considerable detail the requirements of the mortgagor. Some of these common clauses were discussed in a previous section. The main areas of default would be:

- Failure to make your mortgage payments
- Failure to pay your taxes
- Failure to have insurance, or sufficient insurance
- Failure to obey municipal, provincial, or federal law as it relates to the premises that you have mortgaged
- Failure to maintain the premises in habitable condition

- Failure to keep the premises in proper repair
- Deliberately damaging the property that secures the mortgage

2. Mortgagor's Options on Default

If a mortgagor is having difficulty maintaining payments under the mortgage, there are many options to consider. You can:

- Make arrangements with the lender for a waiver of payments for a period of time (for example, three or six months) or arrange for partial payments to be made. This is normally done in a situation where the borrower is sick, injured, or laid off, or has a reduced monthly income to debt-service the mortgage due to a marital separation, a spouse who has been laid off, or other such factors.
- Reschedule the debt and make new payment arrangements.
- Refinance the mortgage with another lender on terms that are more flexible and appropriate in the circumstances.
- Provide additional security to the lender in order to negotiate concessions.
- Put the property up for sale.
- Give the property back to the lender by means of quit claim (transfer of title to the lender) or a similar arrangement.
- Exercise your right of redemption. You are entitled to this by law. This means you pay the arrears outstanding under the mortgage, which prevents the mortgagee from commencing or from continuing foreclosure proceedings. An exception is that if there is an acceleration clause, which most mortgages have, the lender is entitled to deem the full amount of the mortgage immediately due and payable. In that event you would have to pay the full amount of the mortgage in order to stop foreclosure proceedings. In most provinces you have a right of redemption of six months in order to pay the lender, or the lender would be entitled to take over the property, among other remedies.
- Ask the court for more time. If you can see that you are not able to pay off the lender within the six-month right of redemption period, you are entitled to request of the court an extension. The extension could be for an additional three months or six months or longer, and you are entitled to go back to the court to ask for further extensions. Whether the court grants an extension depends on the circumstances. For example, it is in your favour if you had previously lost your job and you are now employed, you are expecting proceeds from an inheritance, or you are having family members raise funds for you. All these are factors that could show that the delay request is based on a realistic assessment of the ability to make the necessary payment. Having a substantial equity in the property would also assist you.

3. Mortgagee's Options on Default

If you are in default and despite all your efforts are unable to come to terms with the lenders, they have various options. Generally the last thing they want to do is take over the property, as there are other remedies that are more appropriate depending on the circumstances. The lenders are required to go to the court and get approval for most of the main remedies available. That gives you an opportunity to present your side of the situation and reveal unique circumstances if you so wish.

Legislation governing the mortgage is provincial and there can be variances between the provinces. For the most part, though, the following remedies would be available to the lender.

- Pay taxes, maintenance fees, or insurance premiums on your behalf. The lender then adds these payments onto your total mortgage debt and charges interest on the amount.
- Obtain an injunction from the court that you stop carrying on some improper or illegal activity. In addition, the order could require you to perform some specific obligation under the mortgage document to protect the mortgage security.
- You would have to pay the lender's costs of obtaining the injunction.
- Take possession of the premises to preserve the mortgage security. This procedure is not often utilized except in serious situations involving revenue properties that are not properly being managed by the borrower.
- Obtain a court order to put the property into receivership. In this case an independent party, called a receiver-manager or receiver, takes possession of the property on behalf of the lender and maintains it. This procedure is rarely appropriate in a residential context and it is usually utilized in the case of revenue property.
- Accelerate the mortgage. The lender has a choice of either requesting the arrears under the mortgage or deeming the full amount of the balance outstanding on the mortgage as immediately due and payable. The lender cannot request this latter course unless there is an acceleration clause in the mortgage.
- Sell the property. This would mean that the lender would be able to put your property up for sale and sell it if you are in default in your payments over a set period of time. The period of time depends on the province. In many cases the lender will go through the court to get a court order for a sale so that the court can monitor the sale price and therefore minimize the risk that the borrower could claim that the house was undersold.
- Sue the borrower personally for the debt outstanding. The liability of the borrower under the terms of the mortgage remains an option for the lender whether or not the property has been sold. If it is sold, the

borrower is responsible for any shortfall. The lender is not required
to commence other actions such as foreclosure or sale of the property.

- Foreclose against the property. In a foreclosure situation, the lender
requests that the court extinguish your rights of redemption and transfer all legal interest that you have, including the right of possession
and legal title, to the lender. In this situation the lender is entitled to
all the equity in the property. The courts have to be involved in this
procedure and your rights are protected in that regard. For example,
the court would consider it inequitable if you had considerable equity
in the property. It would probably advise the lender that instead of
foreclosure there should be an order for sale so that the equity in the
mortgage property would be able to go to the mortgagor after all the
costs associated with the sale, including sales commission, the lender's
legal expenses, and disbursements, plus principal and interest outstanding, were paid off.

As you can see, there are many factors to consider if you are having
financial difficulties on your mortgage. The circumstances of your default
will make a difference in terms of what steps you wish to take. Contacting
the lender and attempting to negotiate a resolution is clearly the first
step that you should take to resolve the problem. If that does not turn
out to be a satisfactory procedure, it would be prudent to obtain advice
from a lawyer specializing in foreclosure matters so that you are fully
aware of your available rights and options.

CHAPTER

4

Timesharing

INTRODUCTION

Resort timesharing originated in Europe in the 1960s, when high costs and demand for limited resort space created the need for a method of assured accommodation for a particular interval of time each year. These intervals are usually sold by the week and include fully furnished accommodation with maintenance and maid service. The concept then moved to Florida in the 1970s to facilitate the sale of the sluggish condominium industry. Since then, timeshares have grown rapidly, with thousands of resorts throughout Canada and the United States and internationally. These resorts range from Ontario cottage country resorts to Colorado ski chalets to Mexican beach villas. Hundreds of thousands of people have purchased timeshares. At some time or other you have probably seen the ads: "Luxury Lifestyle at Affordable Prices!"—"Vacation the World!"—"Trade for Exotic Climes!"—"Buy Your Own Vacation Dream Home!"

The term *timesharing* originated in the computer industry, where clients shared time on expensive computers. Timesharing is now a general term that applies to various methods of purchasing or using vacation homes, condominiums, or motel/hotel accommodation for a certain time period each year. Other terms synonymous with timesharing frequently used include: *resort timesharing, vacation ownership, multi-ownership, interval ownership*, and *shared vacation plan*. The timeshare concept has been applied to numerous other areas: recreational vehicle and mobile home parks, retirement centres, yachts, marinas, cruiseships, and aircraft. (If you are interested in the many forms of timesharing, you may wish to refer to an excellent publication by Anthony Marks entitled *Real Estate Time-Sharing*. (See Appendix B.)

This chapter will discuss the advantages and disadvantages of time-sharing, the types of timesharing plans and time periods, exchange networks, management and legal aspects of timesharing, and how to select a timeshare.

A. ADVANTAGES AND DISADVANTAGES OF TIMESHARING

1. Advantages

(a) There is a potential hedge against impact of inflation on future accommodation prices. The timeshare cost over time could be substantially less than the cost of a rental accommodation that you otherwise would be prepared to pay every year if you were going to the same location. The theory is that once you have a firm contract price, it cannot be increased. You will actually be saving money on accommodations. The reality, though, is that there are additional costs that could be associated with your time purchase. If you are financing the time purchase, you could be paying the debt-servicing cost which could add another 10 to 20% onto your payments. In addition, timeshare projects charge a maintenance fee which is approximately 4% of the total contract price of the timeshare, and this is paid annually. Naturally inflation is going to impact on the factors that make up the maintenance fee, and therefore the fee will increase over time.

(b) You pay only for the period of time that you actually use every year. The cost would therefore be a lot less than if you purchased a condominium or cabin outright, but only used it occasionally during the year.

(c) You are guaranteed the use of a specific motel, suite, or apartment in your chosen resort area for the week or more that you have selected. (However, as will be discussed in later sections of this chapter, there are different types of timeshares, and some do not assure the use of the exact suite every year or at the same time.)

(d) You are permitted to let anyone else use your suite, in most cases by advising the resort management company in advance.

(e) Many resort timesharing facilities are of high quality in terms of their features, furnishings, and construction.

(f) Many resort timeshares have self-contained suites, thereby enabling you to save money on food expenses that would otherwise be incurred by eating at restaurants.

(g) If you have fee simple ownership to your timeshare, or had a lease-hold interest in the timeshare location, you would normally be entitled to sell it at any time if you so wished. There is a commission fee of up to 20% if you use a broker to sell it.

(h) If you purchased a fee simple timeshare interest, over time the value of the interest could increase if you selected a highly desirable location and time period at the outset. There is no guarantee, of course, that there would be any increase in value, because there are many other factors such as an excess of timeshares available in your area, or a depressed market because of the economy, or other factors which could limit interest in any suite for sale privately.

(i) If you have a fee simple timeshare interest, you could rent it out directly or through a rental agent.

(j) If you had a fee simple timeshare interest, you could bequeath your interest in your will to anyone you wish like any other asset.

(k) There are security and safety features. A timeshare interest is protected throughout the year against vandalism because of the ongoing management and maintenance aspect of a timeshare project, even though you may only be using the timeshare for a week a year.

(l) In many cases you can exchange your vacation weeks, depending upon availability and membership provisions, for vacations in any affiliated resort with the exchange network. A nominal exchange fee is paid for this service. Naturally, the interest in exchanging another suite for your suite would be based on the attractiveness of your suite and your timeshare development, and other factors as well.

(m) You can make friends with other interval residents who have similar interests if you go to the same location in the same project every year. A sense of community could therefore be developed.

2. Disadvantages

(a) If you are accustomed to vacationing for extended periods of time such as six to ten weeks a year at a specific location, timesharing would not be an attractive or financially viable alternative.

(b) You may prefer the privacy of a separate vacation spot or a smaller resort.

(c) When you purchase a timeshare, the budget projections that are given to you for annual maintenance fees could have been grossly underestimated by the developer in order to promote sales. Once the real costs start materializing, the timeshare maintenance costs could be too expensive for you.

(d) The developer could get into financial difficulty and the development could be taken over by creditors. This could seriously compromise your timeshare interests and you could lose all your money, and be denied the opportunity to use the timeshare. If you owned a fee simple interest, that would assist your position.

(e) You may have difficulty raising financing on your own if you are unable to pay the full amount of the timeshare costs at the outset. For this reason many timeshare developers carry financing after payment of a down payment. If you had fee simple interest in the timeshare, and you sold the interest, the purchaser may have difficulty getting financing as he or she was not the original timeshare purchaser.

(f) If you have a non-ownership timeshare, in other words, a right-to-use plan, you would either not be able to sell your timeshare interest or would not be able to do so for a profit.

(g) You would not be able to redecorate or furnish the apartment to your taste, as the timeshare project management company or association board of directors would determine the decor.

(h) You may have to pay for recreational facilities and other resort amenities that may be of no interest to you, and may not be compatible with your personal needs. Such facilities as golf courses, tennis courts, and exercise facilities could have operational costs that are included in your annual maintenance fee, whether you like it or not.

(i) If your timeshare period is not during the peak season at an attractive resort, you could have difficulty arranging for an exchange to another timeshare development.

(j) Your timeshare project could be deemed ineligible by a timeshare exchange company if your "home resort" is subsequently rejected by the exchange network due to its not meeting the minimum standards of quality and maintenance, or otherwise not meeting the exchange company's requirements. This could mean that you would be totally unable to be a member of an exchange system, and therefore lose out on that option. That could obviously affect your ability to sell your timeshare interest if you had a fee simple ownership in the timeshare, a situation very similar to that in (i).

(k) In most timeshare projects you are not permitted to bring pets with you.

(l) After taking into account the costs of debt-servicing your timeshare purchase, including principal and interest charges plus increase in maintenance fee due to inflation, you could be paying more for your one-week vacation than other satisfactory alternatives.

B. TYPES OF TIMESHARING PLANS

There are several types of plans, each with its own advantages and disadvantages. It is common for many resorts not to clearly specify in their brochures the type of timesharing plan offered. As mentioned before, the terminology can be very confusing because in many cases it is the concept of timesharing that is marketed rather than the type of timesharing plan.

Depending on your needs, one type of plan may be more appropriate than another. The two common plans are fee simple ownership and right-to-use plans.

1. Fee Simple Ownership

Basically, this type of timeshare involves purchasing an equity ownership in a condominium. There are two variations of these options: estate for years and time-span ownership.

(a) Estate for Years

There are two stages to this type of ownership. In the first, the buyer obtains ownership of the unit for a set number of years, estimated to be the useful life of the building—generally 20 to 40 years. Then at the end of the specified term, the buyer and all other owners of the building become tenants in common of the unit. The undivided share in the resort, property, is based on the person's percentage in the unit, generally 1/50 tenant-in-common interest for each timeshare week. The overall unit then would represent a proportional percentage ownership relative to the total number of units in the project. At this point, the second stage, it is a relationship similar to owning a condominium in a condominium complex, and the factors outlined in the earlier chapters on condominiums would be applicable.

In an estate for years, the purchaser will own and have exclusive use of the condominium unit for the specified week every year for the specified number of years in the agreement. At the end of that time the time-limit guarantee arrangement would terminate and basic ownership would be the same as having a portion ownership in any condominium. At that point the owners could agree to either sign extension agreements or make other plans—for example, to sell the resort and split the profits. This type of fee simple ownership is commonly used in jurisdictions which do not have condominium legislation.

(b) Time-Span Ownership

This type of ownership is based on a tenancy-in-common relationship from the outset. The buyer receives an undivided interest in the whole living unit, based pro rata on the number of weeks selected, but is not given direct priority interest in any specified time period. A separate contractual agreement establishes the right to a particular period. Generally the buyer receives 1/50 tenant-in-common ownership for each week of the timeshare purchased. This is because only 50 weeks would be sold, leaving 2 weeks available for refurbishing and repair. In some cases 51 weeks are sold, leaving 1 week available for renovations or annual cleanup.

(c) Advantages and Disadvantages of Fee Simple Ownership

One of the main advantages of fee simple ownership is the potential value in terms of increase in equity over time if demand develops for your timeshare unit. Another feature is that an ownership interest gives you more say in the ongoing management of the program: you become a voting member of the owners' association which elects directors and retains a management company. In addition, important policy decisions normally require a large majority of the owners to agree before expenses or commitments are made on behalf of the overall project. You may also find it easier to obtain purchase financing by having an equity percentage interest as a tenant in common.

Some people could perceive the responsibility to participate in the affairs of an owners' association as a limiting factor. They would rather enjoy their stay in a facility where the management is responsible for everything rather than having to concern themselves with potential management problems. Another factor is that some people consider the numbered fixed-week basis as being too restrictive in terms of holiday plans and lifestyle. This concern has been modified by the exchange network system that is available with many resorts, but the exchange system does not always guarantee an exchange will occur.

2. Right-to-Use Timesharing Plans

Right-to-use means a non-equity ownership position in the timeshare. It provides you with an occupancy membership in the resort for the specified number of years in the agreement. In other words, you may want to look upon a right-to-use timeshare as the equivalent of a long-term prepaid advance booking of a specific type of accommodation. This type of timeshare allows you occupancy of the vacation accommodation and resort facility for a number of years on a weekly basis. The occupancy rights revert to the resort owner or club at the expiration of the term. Some plans provide you with the option to renew participation at the time of expiration at a price based on an agreed-upon formula or at the original price.

There are many reasons why some resorts are made available only on a right-to-use basis. Some of them are as follows:

- Hotels or motels may find it more practical to convert some of their rooms to timesharing, and leave the rest of the rooms for conventional use. In many cases it would not be feasible for the owner to convert all of the hotel or motel to separate condominium type units. By only allocating a portion of the unit, the necessary flexibility is provided to make timesharing feasible, as cash flow is coming in from the other, non-timeshare part of the operation.

- A hotel or motel may have so many apartments in the building that it would be financially prohibitive to partition the suites for individual ownership as condominium timeshares.

- A developer may find that local zoning or other restrictions prohibit building condominiums, but permit construction for transient housing such as hotels or motels or right-to-use housing.

- The developer may have other plans for the property after the time-share interval use has expired, and therefore wish to retain ownership of the property.

- A country's law or local regulations may prevent ownership. For example, Ireland only permits leases on property, although they can be long-term leases such as for 99 years. And Mexico has regulations that prohibit non-nationals from owning land in many coastal resort areas.

There are three main types of right-to-use timeshares: vacation licence, vacation lease, and club membership.

(a) Vacation Licence

In this type, the buyer has a right to use a selected living unit for a specified week or weeks for a term of years, or for the useful life of the building. You may be permitted to sell your licence in some cases, but you are usually restricted from doing so at a profit. In most cases the licence restricts you from renting out the living unit to someone else. It is common to find vacation licences where timesharing units are being sold in an operating hotel. The reason for the restriction against selling or selling at a profit is that government regulations may require the buyer to be purchasing the timeshare only for his use and enjoyment. Otherwise the sale of the licence could be interpreted as an investment action, and that could be regulated by security legislation.

(b) Vacation Lease

This is similar to the licence plan except that the buyer has a lease on a particular unit and for a fixed occupancy period. In many cases the lease may be transferable to someone else under a sale, and sub-leasing (renting) your timeshare suite under a lease is often acceptable.

(c) Club Membership

In this example the owner has the right to occupy a living space for a specified annual interval. The club is generally a non-profit association similar to a country club that purchases or leases the building or a group of buildings for the benefit of the club members. As with vacation licences, the annual timeshare use period may be selected on a floating basis, or the time period may be fixed.

(d) Advantages and Disadvantages of Right-to-Use Timesharing Plans

Some of the advantages of right-to-use timeshares are as follows:

- The timeshares are usually less expensive to purchase than ownership timeshares.
- The right to use the timeshare will be for fewer years than if you are buying outright, which may be more convenient for your changing lifestyle needs.
- You do not have to become involved in the responsibilities of ownership voting on the affairs of the owners' association and other, related matters.
- The developer has a vested interest in keeping the property in excellent condition because at the end of the timeshare period, all occupancy units revert to the developer.
- Many maintenance budgets have a limit on the potential annual increases based on a cost of living index.
- The legal documentation and costs associated with purchasing a right-to-use timeshare are less than for an ownership timeshare, because of the relative simplicity of the right-to-use format.

Some of the disadvantages are:

- You are not building any potential equity in your financial purchase.
- During your term of use you have no control over the sale of the resort or the selection of the buyer. You should make sure that there is a provision in the original documents you sign that states that if the resort is sold the new owner will honour the remaining time and terms of your timeshare agreement.
- You will have no input on the maintenance and management operations of the resort.
- In order to avoid potential problems under security legislation, and in an attempt to minimize investment speculation assertions by sales personnel, you may be prevented from reselling your timeshare weeks. In other words, you could be locked in or lose your financial outlay. Alternatively, if you are permitted to resell your unit, you could be limited to selling it for the original purchase price so that there would be no risk that the developer could be accused of attempting to present the timeshare as a good investment opportunity.
- The value of your timeshare, if you are able to sell it, is going to depreciate relative to the balance of years left on your right to use agreement.

In summary, the right-to-use timeshare merely provides you with the privilege to occupy one of the units. It generally applies to a type of accommodation rather than a specific unit. You may always be entitled to, for example, a one-bedroom unit with a total occupancy of six and you could always depend on that type of unit, but not necessarily the same unit each time. The right-to-use program has many risks in that the members do not have any ownership interest in the property, but merely a contract requiring the owner of the facility to provide unit accommodation for a long period of time—in many cases up to 30 years or more. Since you do not have any rights as a member to influence the management or operation of the facility, your only recourse, if you are unhappy, is to claim that the developer has failed to meet the minimum standard of service required under the contract. In practical terms this could be expensive and time-consuming, and the outcome could be very uncertain. That is why you should be cautious about purchasing a right-to-use timeshare.

C. TYPES OF TIME PERIODS

There are two types of time periods: fixed time and flexible (flex) time.

1. Fixed Time

This is a very common system, wherein you select one or more specific weeks and the written contract confirms that you are the only occupant entitled to use those time periods. A timeshare unit is normally divided into 52 weeks a year, of which only 50 or 51 weeks are assigned. The week that is provided to you is not based on calendar dates, but on the number of that week in any given year. For example, you could be entitled to the tenth week of the year, with the first week of the year deemed to commence as of a Friday, Saturday, Sunday, or Monday (as most people prefer to commence their holidays on a weekend). The week then runs from Friday to Friday, or Saturday to Saturday, etc. Normally check-in time is the afternoon of the first day, and check-out time in the morning of the last day. That provides a period for cleanup of the unit for the next party. Thus the exact calendar dates are going to vary from year to year.

2. Flexible Time

(a) Floating Time

In the floating-time type of flex time, you normally purchase a timeshare within a price range or season rather than a fixed-week selection. For example, the year could be broken into three basic seasons: summer, spring/fall, and winter. You would have a right to occupancy within the ranges for the price-for-season that you purchased every year on a first-reservation and availability basis. Price differences are based on the demand within each season for that particular facility. It is important to reserve well in advance to ensure availability of the times that you would prefer. Some developers permit members to split their vacation by splitting the week. These are called *split-week plans*. For example, you could reserve four days in August and three days in September.

(b) Open Use

In the open-use type of flex time, you buy a fixed amount of annual timeshare, usually in one-week segments, which you would be entitled to use anytime during the year, subject to availability. In the case of an open-use system the one-week timeshare is normally the same price for anyone, because there is no specific season or week to which you are automatically entitled. It is important to reserve the time well in advance, for there is a stronger demand for desirable holiday periods. Normally the developer will place limitations on the number of times that you would be able to book during the seasonal or holiday periods that are in high demand, in order to be fair to all the timeshare members.

3. Advantages and Disadvantages of Fixed and Flexible Systems

The benefits of the fixed week are that you have the peace of mind of knowing that you can rely on accommodations at a specific week during the year; you can effect exchanges or rentals faster because you have a set week established for your unit, which makes it easier for the exchange network to meet your needs; and your neighbours will generally be the same people every year.

The flexible system provides you with more seasonal variety and greater flexibility; you will seldom see the same neighbours every year, and you could be frustrated by the lack of certainty that you will obtain the time that you request. The longer you take before making up your mind, the fewer vacation dates will be available for you. This could be very frustrating unless you have flexible vacation availability.

D. EXCHANGE NETWORKS

Exchange network companies provide a service whereby you can trade your vacation weeks with others at resorts of similar quality in over a thousand resorts in over 30 countries worldwide. There are over 600,000 members worldwide participating in these types of arrangements.

The exchange system is based on a computer bank of all the available time periods and all the members who are offering their units for trade. Each member is entitled to the same amount of time as deposited in a comparable type of resort, subject to availability. The timeshare companies generally rank your trade on the basis of the quality of the resort, the season, and the weekly period that you have available. In addition, your trade is given a rating relative to the space that it has in terms of numbers of people that your unit could accommodate. Most exchange companies will permit you to select a week different from your own week, but the general rule of thumb is that you can trade the same or trade down, but can't trade up. Also, most resorts and exchange companies allow you to carry credit from year to year if you don't use up your one-week allotment. You could then spend several weeks a few years later, if that was your preference.

In general, the exchange networks work efficiently; approximately 80% of the exchange requests are fulfilled with approximately a 90% satisfaction rate. If an affiliated resort gets continual complaints it will either have to raise its standards or risk being expelled by the exchange company.

1. Types of Exchange Programs

There are three types of exchange systems: external exchanges, internal exchanges, and direct-affiliation exchanges.

(a) External Exchanges
In this type of system, resorts pay an exchange company in order to be on its system. If the timeshare owner in an exchange member resort pays an annual membership fee, he or she may trade accommodations with owners from other resorts who are members of the same exchange company. You are charged a fee for each trade. The two largest exchange companies are Resort Condominiums International and Interval International. You can obtain further information by contacting these companies. (Refer to Appendix A.)

(b) Internal Exchanges
This type of system is operated by developers of multiple resorts and permits trades for accommodations within their corporate network of resorts or affiliated resorts. An exchange fee is usually charged, but there are generally no annual membership fees.

(c) Direct-Affiliation Exchanges
This type involves trades directly between owners using an exchange service. In these types of exchanges, the developer has no involvement or responsibility in the process; it is a personal matter between the owners. There is usually an annual membership fee as well as a charge for each exchange.

2. Advantages and Disadvantages of Exchange Services

Here are some advantages to consider:

- An exchange company monitors the quality of the member resort to make sure that it is complying with the high standards of the network. This helps to keep the developers committed to maintaining the quality of the resort so that they can remain in the network, with all the marketing and financial benefits of that type of arrangement.

- You do not have to vacation at the same resort each year.
- Such services provide flexibility if you are unable to get away for holidays at the same time each year, or at all in a particular year, as you can bank your time.
- They provide flexibility as your vacation lifestyle changes over time, due to such factors as retirement, children leaving home, having more disposable income, etc.
- They provide flexibility if your type of employment causes you to be transferred fairly often, thereby limiting the use that you could obtain from your home resort. You would be able to exchange for a resort area closer to your new location, assuming that your own timeshare is attractive enough that someone would want it.

Some disadvantages you should consider are:

- You cannot accommodate more people in your exchange unit than you could at your home unit. This makes sense, of course; otherwise everyone would attempt to "trade up" and the system would not be fair or workable.
- You cannot exchange to the same resort two years in a row. This, of course, is designed to discourage people who attempt to monopolize the most attractive resorts.
- You cannot exchange your home unit until it is totally ready for occupancy, which, if your home unit is still being constructed, delays for one or two years your access to the exchange system for trade purposes.
- You are responsible for any damage caused by people using your unit on an exchange basis. In practical terms, this would not happen very often, because the offending exchangers could be forbidden from using the exchange in future.
- If your home resort has financial difficulties and goes into bankruptcy, or does not meet the minimum standards of the exchange, your resort would be delisted and you would not be able to have any exchange privileges.
- Exchange opportunities could be reduced considerably if owners of units that were in prime weeks or locations decided to rent out their units rather than exchange them.

E. TIMESHARE RESALES

If you are buying a timeshare with the intention of reselling it at some point in the future, you should be very selective about the type of timeshare that you purchase. If you have purchased a fee simple ownership timeshare and you have an estate-for-years or time-span ownership, you should be able to sell your interest with limited, if any, restrictions.

If you have a right-to-use timeshare, then, as mentioned earlier, you could have considerable difficulty in reselling your membership. In many cases you do not have a right to resell, or there are considerable restrictions on resale rights, such as the requirement of the club's approval, or the right of first refusal for the club to buy it back from you, or a restriction that you cannot sell your membership for any more than you paid for it. In other words, you cannot make a profit.

The resale of your timeshare interest is handled in a fashion similar to that of selling a home. There are basically four ways of selling the timeshare.

1. Private Sale

You can attempt to sell your timeshare interest privately by posting a notice on the bulletin board of the resort, putting an ad in the classified section of the newsletter or newspapers, or through word of mouth.

2. Sale through Developer

Some timeshare developers also provide a resale service through their sales office. Naturally, there has to be an incentive for developers; otherwise they would prefer to sell their own timeshares, because there would be a higher profit margin. The developer will ask for a commission which is normally 20% of the sales price.

3. Sale through a Real Estate Broker

You can list your timeshare with various real estate brokers. The commission could be between 10 and 20%, in other words higher than in selling a home, because the selling price is considerably lower than in selling a house and it could take a lot more effort to sell the timeshare.

4. Sale through a Timeshare Broker Company

Because of the large number of timeshares, there has been a considerable growth in the resale market, and many timeshare broker companies have been established. You can obtain a list of the timeshare resale companies from the National Timeshare Council. (Refer to Appendix A.)

F. MANAGEMENT OF TIMESHARES

Once you have purchased a timeshare, that gives you the basic occupancy right, and, if you have a fee simple interest, also an ownership. You will have ongoing expenditures relating to the timeshare, and these are covered under a maintenance fee and occupancy fee which reflect your share of the operating and management expenses. Over time and with approximately 50 timeshare users spending a week each in the same unit, there could be considerable wear and tear. The unit may have to be repainted and repaired and the furniture replaced, and also the appliances from time to time. Developers plan on redoing the units every three, five, or seven years. In practical terms, many developers will replace as the circumstances require in order to maintain the standards and quality of the resort, and to comply with the requirements of the exchange company. As mentioned earlier, one or two weeks a year are unsold and set aside for refurbishing. The management company, acting for the developers or the unit owners, is responsible for setting aside a contingency reserve for replacement and refurbishing purposes. This could be 10 to 20% of your total maintenance fee. Many other items are covered by the maintenance fee, including upkeep and maintenance of the other amenities at the resort—for example, the swimming pool and the exercise facilities—and larger expenses such as real estate taxes and utilities, major restorations, and the management operation fee.

If you are purchasing in a new timeshare project, the developer will provide an itemized budget of anticipated annual operating costs for the project. These will be broken down into a share of those costs per one-week interval. As to the accuracy of the projections, if the developers have been involved in other timeshare projects, they should have a fairly realistic idea of the type of expenses that would be incurred. As discussed earlier, some developers intentionally give an artificially low budget in order to make the timeshare an attractive purchase because of possible sales resistance if the maintenance fees were perceived as being too high. The problem, of course, is that once the timeshare is operational, the fees for maintenance could skyrocket.

Most timeshare programs charge you a maintenance fee regardless of whether you use your facility or not that year. Especially in the case of right-to-use programs, the maintenance fee is like annual membership dues that have to be paid. In addition, some right-to-use programs have a provision that, if you failed to use your time in any particular year, they would have a right to rent out the unit without paying you any benefit.

In the case of fee simple ownership plans, the owners hire the management firm, and therefore have control. In the case of a right-to-use plan, you do not have any control over the management company, as the developers employ the management company for their own needs and purposes, and pass on the expenses to you as part of your contractual obligations.

In a typical operating budget for a timeshare project, the following are the types of maintenance fees, occupancy fees, and real estate taxes usually found.

Maintenance Fees

- Accounting
- Annual unit maintenance (painting, wallpapering, etc.)
- Association meetings and expenses
- Cablevision
- Electricity (common areas)
- Gas (on barbecue)
- Insurance
- Lawn maintenance
- Maintenance service and supplies
- Management fee
- Occupational licence
- Office supplies and postage
- Payroll and related taxes
- Pest control
- Reserve for maintenance and repairs
- Reserve for depreciation
- Telephone
- Waste disposal
- Water and sewer (common areas)

Occupancy Fees

- Books, magazines, newspapers
- Cleaning supplies (weekly)
- Electricity (for individual unit)
- Maid service (weekly)
- Water and sewer (for individual unit)

Real Estate Taxes

Keep in mind that operating budgets will vary considerably from project to project, depending on the size of the overall resort, common area amenities, individual unit size, climate, level of service provided, local labour costs, taxes, and other factors. Make sure you receive a detailed copy of the operating budget and review and understand it in advance. Be wary of timeshare programs that guarantee that the maintenance fee will not go up during the first few years. This could mean that the developer is underwriting operating losses and as soon as the guarantee period ends, the maintenance fees will rise very quickly due to the hidden costs that were previously covered, plus inflationary pressure.

G. LEGAL ASPECTS OF TIMESHARING

There are many legal considerations that you have to take into account
in buying a timesharing unit. The following sections discuss some of the
factors to consider:

1. Legislation

Because the timeshare industry is relatively new and rapidly expanding,
many provinces and states do not have any legislation dealing specifically
with timeshares. Real estate is a provincial and state responsibility, so
no federal agency in Canada or the United States has legislation. Also,
the legislation that exists is always changing and evolving. Therefore, in
many cases the advice "Let the buyer beware" is highly appropriate—
though some provinces and states have consumer protection legislation
dealing with timeshares, as will be discussed later in this section.

2. Timeshare Councils

Both Canada and the United States have timeshare councils. These are
self-regulatory bodies of the respective timeshare industries and comprise
the resort timesharing developers, marketing agencies, and professional
and consulting firms. The council in each country sets standards of ethics
and conduct and attempts to help the industry develop in an organized
and orderly fashion.

In Canada, the council is called the Resort Timesharing Council of
Canada and in the United States it is called the National Timeshare Council. (Refer to Appendix A for contact addresses and phone numbers.)

Membership in these councils does not assure the purchaser of a timeshare of the value of the purchase, but it does indicate that the member
company has stated that, in order to protect the public, it will adhere to
the high standards set by the council and abide by the code of ethics. So
if you are having problems with a timeshare developer that is a member
of a council, it will provide you with some opportunity to pressure the
developer to resolve the problems.

The following is an overview of the code of ethics which members of
the Canadian or United States timeshare councils are supposed to adhere
to.

- Members shall make honesty and integrity the standard in all their
  commerce, whether representations are oral or written. They pledge
  to avoid misleading descriptions, concealment of pertinent information, and exaggeration in advertising.
- Members shall make no false, misleading, or extravagant claims with
  respect to any timeshare project.

- Members shall endeavour to ensure wherever possible that any prospective purchaser makes an on-site inspection. In any event, they shall be certain that the customer has received full, accurate, and complete disclosure of all pertinent information relating to the security given and to the project generally.

- Members shall also offer the timeshare buyer the option of rescinding his purchase within a specific time limit that is of sufficient duration to allow for and encourage inspection. They shall instruct their sales staff and agents to observe this code and to recognize the customer's interests.

- Members shall express financial and contractual obligations in written documents that comply with all applicable laws.

- Members shall not deny a person the right to acquire any timeshare interest because of race, sex, colour, creed, religion, or national origin.

- Members shall make suitable financial arrangements to ensure completion of timeshare projects in their entirety.

- Members shall plan, design, and build their developments in compliance with all laws, ordinances, and regulations applicable thereto.

- Members shall conduct all business affairs with dignity and propriety. They shall avoid conflicts of interest and shall promote integrity as the highest ideal to be followed by all their employees.

- Members shall adhere to the highest ideals of moral conduct in all their business relations. At no time shall an inducement of profit justify departure from this code or from honourable business standards.

3. Fee Simple Ownership Timeshare

As discussed earlier, the purchase of a timeshare by means of ownership as part-owner of a condominium has the same precautions as buying any condominium unit in terms of the documentation and procedures. Refer to the section on legal considerations in purchasing a condominium in the chapter on legal aspects (Chapter 2). Additional documents could be required, including a separate agreement for specified usage in terms of a specific period of time during the year.

The type of documentation that you should receive to review before purchasing the timeshare condominium would include copies of the owners' association (equivalent to condominium corporation) articles, rules and regulations, management agreement, estimate of annual maintenance expenses, purchase and sale agreement, and agreement relating to time of usage. Generally you will have a lawyer who will be doing the closing on your behalf, to protect your interests, and have the documents filed in the land registry offices.

4. Right-to-Use Timeshare

This type of timeshare merely gives the right to occupy the premises by means of lease, licence, or club membership. You do not have any ownership rights whatsoever in the property. Therefore, the legal documentation is a lot simpler than for fee simple ownership, and the closing costs are far less. Generally you do not use a lawyer at all, but simply sign documents which set out the relationship between you and the developer. The documents are not filed against the property as they would be with a fee simple ownership; there may be exceptions in the case of a timeshare lease arrangement.

5. Recision Option

Most provinces and states have consumer protection legislation which allows a cooling-off or *recision period*, by which you have the opportunity to change your mind for any reason about purchasing a product, and to ask for all your money back without any deductions or penalty. Recision periods can vary from three to thirty days.

It is important to keep in mind that the recision period is effective only in the jurisdiction where you make the purchase. If you purchase a timeshare in California, your recision rights would be governed by California law even though you live in Ontario. The number of days that you have to rescind the contract is based on the calendar, and they commence from the date that you signed the agreement. It is important to keep this in mind if you are holidaying outside Canada, because you could lose your recision rights if you do not consider rescinding the contract until after you get home and the period has elapsed. Certain states, and many countries, do not have recision periods (for example, Mexico).

If you are purchasing a timeshare in a jurisdiction that does not have recision rights, individual developers may incorporate the right of recision within the purchase agreement. Other development companies may extend the recision period longer than required by law to show their good faith and confidence in the quality of their resort timeshare program. Check to make sure that your recision rights, either by contract or by law, are clearly outlined in the purchase documentation. If you do rescind, you have to do so in writing, and the developer has to receive the notice before the deadline. For your protection, make sure that you have proof of delivery either by courier or by hand delivery, and obtain a receipt; that is very important in the event of a dispute as to whether you cancelled within the recision period.

6. Waiver of Right of Partition

Under the legislation of the provinces, and most states as well, there is a provision for partition and sale of a property which is held under tenancy in common. For example, if there were 50 people as tenants in common holding 1/50 each of interest in a condominium timeshare unit, and one of those people decided to sell his interest and was not able to do so, he could make an application in court to force a sale of the condominium and then obtain 1/50 of the net proceeds of the sale. In most cases you would not know any of the other owners of a timeshare unit, and therefore there could be a risk that someone could commence that action. This would certainly compromise your interest in the condominium, and could defeat your whole purpose in investing in the resort unit. To avoid problems, it is important to have a waiver of partition rights under the laws of the particular province or state concerned. When you are purchasing a fee simple condominium timeshare unit, you should make sure that this is clearly stated in the agreement before you sign any documentation. In other words, the agreement would state that all the tenants in common of that particular unit were agreeing not to exercise any partition rights.

If you are buying a right-to-use timeshare, you do not have to be concerned about the partition issue, because you do not own any right to the property in that situation.

7. Independent Escrow Account

Many provinces and states require that developers hold any money paid to them as a down payment or full payment in trust in a separate account called an *escrow* account until the recision period is over. You would not receive any interest on your money, but if you decide to cancel the agreement, you would get all the money back. If you are buying into a new project which has not been completed, you may want to protect your funds by having them go into an escrow account with the condition that they cannot be released until such time as the project is complete. You could negotiate interest on the deposit funds to the credit of your account, though many developers would not agree to this provision easily because they would like to use your funds for the project's completion. On the other hand, lending companies will finance a development project on the strength of the amount of money held in the trust or escrow account as down payment. Always consider the risk of the developer's going into bankruptcy or having financial problems and the project not completing, when you are making a down payment on an uncompleted project. If that happens, unless you have protected yourself at the outset you would have lost your deposit monies. Although you would be entitled to sue the developer, in practical terms it could mean wasted money in legal fees, as well as being expensive, stressful, time-consuming, uncertain in outcome, and lengthy before resolution. You would also have the additional problem, if you are living outside the jurisdiction of the timeshare, of the expense of having to appear in court. Developers, of course, would be aware of this fact; and development companies are limited-liability corporations. They would realize that if the deposit is not too large, you will probably write off the loss and not pursue the matter.

8. Requirement to Honour Timeshare Agreement in Foreclosure

If you have a fee simple interest in a condominium timeshare and the project has financial difficulties or goes into bankruptcy, you would have certain very clear rights in law with regard to your equity interest in the unit. On the other hand, if you have a right-to-use timeshare and the membership club or resort goes into bankruptcy and another development company takes over the timeshare resort, you could lose all your entitlement under the right-to-use agreement. One way around this problem is to ensure that there is a provision in the documentation you sign that binds the holder of the mortgage to honour any timesharing agreements in the event of foreclosure. This may be difficult to obtain, but it is a point that you should consider and investigate.

9. Legal Advice

It is prudent to get legal advice in any timeshare purchase situation. Ideally you should speak to a lawyer in the jurisdiction in which the timeshare is located and seek an opinion from a lawyer who has expertise in real estate in general and timeshares in particular. You can contact the local bar association or lawyer referral service in the area of the timeshare, and ask for the name of the lawyer who is expert in real estate timeshares. You can also consult the local Yellow Pages under "Lawyers," looking at the specialty areas mentioned, and contact several lawyers on the phone to see if they have expertise in the area of timeshares. Then you could set up an appointment for a half-hour consultation. Make sure that you have all the documentation you have received from the timeshare company—which you should not have yet signed—for the lawyer to review. If the lawyer has expertise in real estate timeshares, it should not take more than half an hour to review the documentation and give you an opinion on the key areas to be wary of. In addition, the lawyer would probably know the reputation and track record of the resort in that area, which could be of assistance to you. The costs for a half-hour consultation would be between $50 and $100. This is not much money to pay for your peace of mind and legal protection.

If you are buying a right-to-use timeshare, no lawyers need to be involved, because the paperwork is very simple. Normally all the documents are signed between the purchaser and the sales agents for the developer at their place of business. Having the documentation reviewed by a lawyer would be prudent, however.

On the other hand, if you are buying a fee simple ownership in a condominium timeshare unit, you require a lawyer to represent your interests and to complete the transaction. You should use the same lawyer that you selected to review the documentation in advance and advise you, before you sign any binding offer to purchase or other documentation. The legal costs and disbursements for closing the purchase of a fee simple ownership could range between $300 and $750 or more depending on the price and complexity of your purchase.

H. HOW TO SELECT A TIMESHARE

The first thing you have to do is to determine your vacation needs, so that you have some idea of the type of timeshare that you may wish to consider. Once you have done this, there are many other factors that you have to consider when selecting a specific timeshare. These two steps are discussed in the next sections.

1. Determining Your Vacation Needs

It is important to determine, and if applicable to discuss with your family, what you really enjoy in a vacation in the light of your prior experiences and needs. Sort out your priorities so that you can have the confidence that your decision to purchase a timeshare resort is a good one. Here are some questions to evaluate:

- How frequently do you take a vacation? (Once a year, more than once a year, occasionally, or seldom)
- How long do you spend on your vacation? (One week, two weeks, a month, or longer)
- What time of year do you prefer to take your vacation? (Spring, summer, fall, winter, specific months)
- Do you enjoy taking vacation in a wide variety of locations? A few locations? Or just one location?
- What type of location appeals to you? (The beach, mountains, lakes, urban or rural areas, etc.)
- What do you prefer to do on your location? (Shopping, sightseeing, nightlife, recreational activity, resting, etc.)
- How much money do you normally spend for accommodations per week on your vacation? (Inexpensive/budget prices, moderate prices, expensive prices)
- How far do you travel on your vacations? (Close to home, a few hours away, one day of travelling, etc.)
- How do you normally travel to your vacation spot? (Car, bus, train, plane, boat, etc.)

- How flexible are your vacation goals? (Long-range planning, last-minute flexibility, structured or unstructured vacation, flexibility in holiday time available, etc.)
- How many people will be accompanying you on vacation? (Single, couple, children, relatives, friends, etc.)
- What kind of people do you prefer to associate with on your vacation?

It is important to look back on the pattern of previous years in terms of the nature, expense, and frequency of your vacations. You should also project future changes in your vacation needs. Assuming that all the other factors favour a timeshare vacation, if the purchase price can be compared favourably to the total cost you would otherwise face for accommodation during the same period of time, timeshares can be a financially attractive decision. You may reach a break-even point on the cost of your timeshare when it is spread over a period from seven to fourteen years, assuming that you are going to use the timeshare during all those years. Naturally you have to take into account inflation factors when trying to equate the monies that you would otherwise spend, the interest that you may be paying on the financing of your timeshare plan, and the cost of annual maintenance of your timeshare. The inflationary impact on those maintenance costs is an additional factor. It is important to sit down with pen and paper and make some very concrete financial projections based on realistic assumptions.

2. Selecting a Timeshare

Be cautious when deciding to purchase a timeshare because of the financial and personal commitment that is involved. You want to make sure that you do not suffer from "buyer's remorse." Here is a summary of the tips and cautions to consider before you make a final decision.

(a) First, determine your vacation needs as outlined above. You want to make sure, before attending any sales presentation, that you are clearly focussed on your needs so that you do not purchase a timeshare impulsively and end up regretting it.

(b) Compare the costs of the timesharing project to costs of similar accommodations in the same area and during the same time of the year.

(c) Compare the costs of other timeshare projects in the resort area that you are considering. Most resort areas that are attractive to tourists have more than one timeshare project in the vicinity. Compare such factors as: the amenities available, the proximity of the project to other amenities in the geographic area that are important to you (entertainment, beaches, etc.), price, maintenance fees, ownership vs. right-to-use timeshares, etc.

(d) Don't buy a timeshare unit with expectations of making a profit on your investment. This can be very risky for many reasons. A large number of timeshare projects could be built over the years in that area, which means that the supply could be considerable and therefore the value of any resale of a fee simple ownership condominium timeshare could actually be reduced. You should consider timesharing more as an opportunity to save money over the years and as a plan which meets your vacation needs as you project them over the next 10 to 15 years, taking the various factors into consideration that have been discussed earlier. Consider the alternatives as well; for example, if you purchase a $20,000 Canada Savings Bond rather than a $20,000 timeshare, you would be receiving interest every year of approximately $1,800 to $2,000 or more. That amount of interest every year could pay for a very memorable vacation at a resort and you would still be keeping the principal amount of the CSBs as an asset. Remember that the timeshare just covers accommodation, and not your transportation costs.

(e) Know the type of timeshare that you are buying. In other words, know whether you are buying a fee simple ownership or a right-to-use timeshare. Be fully aware of the advantages and disadvantages of each so that you can make an informed decision.

(f) Make sure that you know whether the timeshare you are buying is a fixed-week or flexible-week timeshare.

(g) Make sure that you visit the property, if at all feasible. It is difficult to make important financial commitments and personal decisions on the basis of a sales presentation or promotional material. Talk to other timeshare owners in the resort if it is already operating and make enquiries as to their satisfaction. It is important that you enjoy the surrounding environment and related factors. If possible, ask the developer if you can stay at the resort for a few days for free or at a nominal fee, before you finalize your decision.

(h) Check the reputation of the developer. You can do this by contacting the local Better Business Bureau and Chamber of Commerce. In Canada and the United States you can also make enquiries of provincial or state consumer complaint agencies about the developer or about the sales representation.

(i) Check the reputation of the management company. The experience and quality of management will make all the difference as to whether your purchase will be a satisfactory or an unsatisfactory one. Speaking to other timeshare owners in an existing project will provide some feedback. In addition, make enquiries and obtain information about the previous track record of the management company in terms of other timeshare projects they have worked on, how long they have been in business, references, etc. Also contact the owners' association and ask very candid questions. Find out the length of the management contract. If the management contract is renewable on a year-by-year or every-other-year basis, that gives an opportunity to fire the management company and hire a replacement if they are not performing. On the other hand, if the management contract is for an extended period of time (for example, ten years) because the management company is associated with the developer in some fashion, that can be a limiting factor. Physically inspect the resort property, looking for signs of effective management. Are the grounds well kept? Is the office staff polite? Are the facilities well maintained?

(j) Be sure that the unit is sufficient for your needs in terms of features and square footage.

(k) Don't buy a timeshare for the exchange privilege. It is important that you buy the timeshare for its intrinsic benefits. Otherwise, if the developer is no longer part of the exchange network, or if the exchange network is not offering the satisfaction in terms of exchange service to you, then you could be very disappointed in your purchase. You should consider the exchange feature as an extra benefit and not as the sole reason for purchasing. As discussed earlier, there are advantages and limitations to the exchange system.

(l) Make sure you know your legal rights. Make sure that all the representations made by the sales person and the developer are in writing. Ideally, have a lawyer who is knowledgeable about real estate law and timesharing in the jurisdiction of the timeshare give you an opinion. Remember that representations that are spelled out clearly in the sales contract and other documents are all you have to rely on.

(m) Don't be pressured into signing agreements and making a down payment. Of course, many sales people exert all their skills to closing the sale right then and there, because their commission is based on completing a sale. Some resort timeshare area techniques can be very hard-sell and you should be very wary of the techniques that would be used to try to get you to sign quickly. Mexico is one area that you have to be particularly concerned about, because there you do not have the recision rights and other protections that would be available to you in many provincial and state jurisdictions.

(n) Know how long your recision period is—the time period available to you to cancel the agreement and have all the money returned to you. It varies from province to province and state to state, but in most cases it is required by law. The recision period should be clearly stated in the contractual documentation. Also make sure that you decide about the timeshare within the recision period and notify the developer in writing to protect yourself.

(o) Get complete copies of all documentation and give yourself an opportunity to review these in advance. This means all the by-laws, rules and regulations, and other procedures, restrictions, and rights and obligations.

(p) Make sure that you understand the financing arrangements completely. It is important to know who is financing you, whether it be the developer or another lender. Make sure you know how much interest you are going to be charged, whether you can prepay the loan without penalty, the length of term of the loan, and the monthly amount of payments. Negotiate for an attractive interest rate, or else consider obtaining bank financing—or maybe even reconsider the whole timeshare project and consider others.

(q) Make sure that your down payment or full payment on the timeshare is held in escrow. Your money should be held in a bank or with a lawyer, or some other secure escrow account, until the recision period has expired or been waived, or until a newly constructed development is operational. In many jurisdictions, payments are required to be held in escrow until a certain percentage of the project is sold out, or the project is able to be occupied.

(r) Review the disclosure statement and make sure that any holder of a mortgage is required to honour the timeshare agreements in place at the time of any foreclosure.

(s) Obtain a copy of the proposed maintenance budget so that you can see the breakdown of expenses, and the percentage allocated for reserve and for other replacement matters.

(t) If you are purchasing a timeshare in a project which is not yet completed, make sure that you obtain a written commitment from the developer that the facilities will be completed as promised, or if not, that you have the right to obtain your deposit monies back plus interest.

(u) Know what your rights are if the development encounters any financial problems.

(v) Know what the rights of the developers would be if the owners or timeshare right-to-use members do not honour their purchase or maintenance obligations.

(w) Make sure you understand what amenities are included in the maintenance fees and which are extra. Many resorts have a *user pay* policy, whereby the people who use the facilities have to pay for them. In this event, maintenance fees do not automatically cover the facilities; otherwise people would be paying for facilities which they do not use and have no intention of using.

(x) Look at the selling pattern of the units. There is a risk if all the most attractive high-season units are being sold first, because once they are sold out, there could only be low-season, and relatively unattractive, units remaining. This could mean increased maintenance costs as there are fewer people to pay their portion of the maintenance costs of the facility. The developers may have a provision that they do not have to pay an equal amount for unrented timeshares and the existing timeshare members or owners are the ones who are obliged to debt-service all maintenance costs.

(y) Check to make sure that the resort belongs to either the Resort Timesharing Council of Canada or the National Timeshare Council. Make a direct enquiry to see if any complaints have been made against the developer or resort. (See Appendix A.)

CHAPTER

5

Co-operatives

INTRODUCTION

Co-operatives are frequently confused with condominiums and 99-year leases. In outward appearance, they are similar types of accommodation, but the legal differences and the equity interests acquired by the purchaser are very different. This chapter discusses the differences between profit and non-profit co-operatives, the advantages of co-op housing, an overview of the Canadian Co-operative Housing structure, the types of people who are attracted to co-operative housing, how co-operatives are financed, and how to become a co-op member.

A. WHAT IS A CO-OPERATIVE?

Housing co-operatives are groups of people that have joined together to provide their own housing through joint ownership. There are two forms of co-operatives: profit and non-profit. Most co-operatives in Canada, and the type that are eligible for assistance under the Federal Co-operative Housing Program, are non-profit co-operatives. A brief description of the two forms follows. The rest of this chapter discusses in more detail the non-profit form.

1. Co-operative for Profit

In this type of co-operative, a corporation is generally formed under the provincial Company Act. The corporation buys and owns the land and building including all of the units or builds a new building. Each purchaser in the co-operative becomes a shareholder of the corporation. The shareholder who occupies the unit, therefore, is not owner of an interest in land which his or her unit represents. The corporation that owns the property is the party that owns the land and buildings.

The purchase of shares entitles the shareholder (co-operative member) to enter into a lease with the corporation. The lease itself generally contains provisions relating to the payment of a monthly charge. This is not rent as such, but it is equivalent to rent. These payments are equivalent to all costs of operating the lands and buildings and are adjusted as these costs change. The member pays a portion of all costs which reflects the percentage of shares that the member has in the corporation.

The lease between the corporation and the member will generally have provisions relating to use, alterations, repairs, damage, destruction, sale, disputes, and resolution of differences. The lease may also include rules and regulations similar to those in condominium developments. In addition, many co-operatives require all members to sign a shareholders' agreement. This would set out the rights and responsibilities of the member (shareholder) relative to other shareholders in the corporation. Included in the agreement would be such provisions as:

- How the corporation is to be operated
- Financing requirements by shareholders
- Restrictions of transfer of shares by the shareholder
- Right of first refusal of the corporation to buy the shareholder's interest at a fair market value
- Formula for determining the fair market value of a share in the event that the shareholder wishes to sell
- Basis for compulsory buy-out of the shareholder by the corporation
- How a member's share is to be dealt with in the event of death of the member
- The rights of the corporation against the shareholder in the event of default by the latter
- Other provisions

In addition, the member is also affected by the documents of incorporation—specifically, by the articles or by-laws of the corporation. These may contain provisions dealing with sale of the whole building, and transference of shares. It is fairly common to find provisions in the corporate documents restricting share transfers at the discretion of the directors of the corporation. In contrast, the condominium unit owner is free to sell his unit at any time without consulting other members of the condominium corporation.

Mortgage financing for the co-operative is obtained by securing the land and building as a whole, with the corporation as the mortgagor. Each member contributes an amount toward the monthly payment under the mortgage proportional to his or her equity or share interest in the corporation. If a member defaults in payment, the other members will have to ensure that sufficient funds are raised to make the monthly payment or risk foreclosure by the mortgage company. Members would have the right of legal action and a claim against the defaulting member. If several members default on their monthly payment obligations, this can cause a severe burden on the other members of the co-operative. Another consideration is that some lenders may request personal guarantees of the shareholders of the corporation as collateral security to the corporate mortgage. This would provide extra protection to the lender in the event that property values decrease and a foreclosure situation occurs with a resultant shortfall to the bank. This potential or contingent liability on the part of the shareholder requires serious consideration. Make sure you obtain independent legal advice. Limiting the amount of the personal guarantee to the shareholder's percentage interest is one way of limiting the risk, of course. You may prefer not to sign a personal guarantee under any circumstances.

If you are considering getting involved in a co-operative for profit, there are several other factors that you should consider. You might find it very difficult to raise money on the basis of your share interest in the corporation. This could be because the lease that you have with the corporation for your specific unit may not be registered. This would make it difficult or impossible for a lender to register a mortgage against your lease interest. If the lease is registered, the mortgage company would be able to obtain a registered mortgage of lease, but they would probably also want to have your shares in the corporation pledged to them. In that event, if the mortgage company foreclosed, it would become a member (shareholder) of the corporation. Co-operative units are sold frequently on an all-cash basis; however, there could be difficulty in reselling your unit if you required "all cash" without "taking back" a promissory note for part of the purchase price.

Of course, one of the key benefits of a co-operative set up for profit is the potential return on your investment. For example, if you paid $50,000 for your share interest, five years later an increase in land value and market demand may have caused your share equity to be worth $150,000. You would have a capital gain of $100,000. A portion of this gain could be taxable in your hands depending on existing tax legislation and your specific personal tax circumstances; but on the other hand, if you owned a single-family home or a condominium with title under your name as a principal residence, you would be exempt from any capital gain tax on resale regardless of increase in value of the land and building. As you can see, many considerations have to be taken into account when deciding about co-operatives for profit. The administration and management of these types of co-ops is usually done by a board of directors under the Company Act, supplemented by paid or voluntary managers and staff.

2. Non-profit Co-operatives

Non-profit co-operatives are associations incorporated under provincial co-operative or society legislation. They exist primarily to provide housing for their members. These co-operatives are referred to as non-profit because members do not own their housing individually, and are not entitled to sell their membership at a profit. Thus, they do not have the opportunity to realize a capital gain. A member may leave such a co-operative and be replaced by a new member, but the housing is still owned by the association. Co-ops are member-controlled organizations, and the people who occupy the housing owned by the co-operative corporation are its members. Unlike tenants in a traditional rental situation, each member has one vote in the operation of the co-op. Every year, the members elect, from among themselves, a board of directors to manage the business and affairs. Instead of rent, members pay a monthly housing charge to cover the costs of mortgage, taxes, and all operating expenses. Members purchase a share in the co-operative corporation at a reasonable or nominal fee at the outset, and if leaving the co-op, they sell the share back to the corporation or another party at the original cost. A member then has a lease for a specific dwelling.

In a non-profit co-operative there is no landlord, and housing charges rise only as costs increase. A membership in the co-op means joint ownership of the corporation and control of one's housing. From the inception of the co-op, the members decide on design, development, and policy. Once the co-op is operational, they serve on committees responsible for activities like selection of members, finance, maintenance, and newsletters. Any member can run for election to the board of directors. All members are asked to attend members' meetings, where they participate in major decisions. Staff or other professionals may be hired to handle certain problems or routine duties, but the final decisions and responsibilities rest with the members. Members are governed by the by-laws and rules and regulations of the co-op.

As will be discussed later, financing for non-profit co-operatives is provided by the federal government through CMHC under the National Housing Act. In addition, some provinces assist in financing non-profit co-operatives.

B. OVERVIEW OF THE CANADIAN CO-OPERATIVE HOUSING STRUCTURE

The non-profit co-operative housing movement in Canada comprises many types of groups. It includes a national organization of housing co-operatives; provincial, regional, and local organizations which develop new co-operatives and provide services to existing ones; associations of people employed by co-operatives; and individual housing co-operatives.

1. The Co-operative Housing Foundation of Canada (CHF)

The Co-operative Housing Foundation is the national association of non-profit housing co-operatives and their support organizations. CHF's mandate is to support the development of non-profit housing co-operatives in Canada, and to ensure the viable operation of existing housing co-operatives. CHF was founded in 1968 by the Canadian Labour Congress, the Co-operative Union of Canada, and the Canadian Union of Students, which along with several co-operative bodies and the United Church of Canada, are CHF's sponsoring members. CHF's aim is to assist in meeting people's housing needs through the promotion and development of non-profit co-operative housing which the occupants own and control. One of the goals in promoting the co-operative housing sector is to have about 10% of Canada's housing starts produced by co-operatives. CHF also represents and protects the interests of housing co-operatives before governmental bodies and housing authorities, through advocacy at all levels of government and liaison with the CMHC.

The services provided by CHF to developing and existing co-operatives include technical consultation with co-op development groups, creation of co-op management educational materials, staff and volunteer instructor training, management and financial consulting, financial assistance, production of a quarterly newsletter, conferences, seminars, and educational programs, and bulk purchasing of services such as insurance. CHF publishes a comprehensive national directory which is available for purchase.

2. Provincial Confederations

Provincial confederations exist in several provinces, including Ontario and Quebec. They act as vehicles for information sharing and provincial political action on issues affecting the co-operative housing sector. The Co-operative Housing Association of Ontario represents Ontario resource groups, co-operative housing federations, and staff federations. In Quebec, co-operative housing resource groups and federations have developed differently. The resource groups are organized into six associations which liaise through the Coordination nationale des GRT.

3. Co-operative Housing Federations

Co-operative housing federations are local associations of housing co-operatives. The federations train co-operative members to manage their projects independently, and provide them with several consultative services. There are 18 federations of housing co-operatives across Canada. For contact addresses, refer to Appendix A.

4. Co-operative Housing Resource Groups

Co-operative housing resource groups help people to organize and develop non-profit housing co-operatives locally. The development of large housing projects is a complex task that can take years. Resource groups provide specialized technical assistance throughout the development process. Services provided by resource groups fall into two broad categories: membership development and property development. In some areas one organization acts as both a resource group and a federation. Contact the federation closest to you to obtain contact addresses for resource groups.

5. Housing Co-operatives

Housing co-operatives are autonomous corporations established under provincial legislation in which each member/resident is entitled to one vote in the co-operative's decision-making process. To obtain contact numbers for co-operatives in your area, refer to the Yellow Pages under "Co-operatives," or contact a co-operative housing federation.

6. Staff Associations

Staff associations are organizations of people hired by housing co-operatives. These include the coordinators who oversee the general management of projects, and the administrative, cleaning, and maintenance staff.

C. WHO LIVES IN NON-PROFIT CO-OPERATIVE HOUSING?

There are many types of people who prefer the co-op housing option. It is open to all income levels in all segments of society. The membership generally falls into the following categories:

- Senior citizens who prefer selling their homes so that they can move into more suitable rental accommodations for their needs with controlled monthly charges and security of tenure
- People who are unable to buy their own homes
- People faced with escalating rents
- People concerned with the insecurity of the rental market

- People who are accustomed to renting but who would prefer to have direct input about their housing

- People who are on a long waiting list for public housing, or who are in an area where no new public housing is proposed in the foreseeable future

- People who are saving to buy a home and in the meantime desire to live in housing, and like the fact that they have a share in the corporation with rents that are based on actual costs rather than market demand

- Low-income and disadvantaged people who have little bargaining power or choice under normal market conditions

- People who philosophically prefer the co-operative housing option environment

In non-profit co-operatives, there are no income qualifications for any individual. However, the co-operative as a group generally has a mix of incomes which allows them to meet the expenses, and which may include high and moderate as well as low income. In many cases the members will pay 25 to 30% of their gross income up to a ceiling established by the lower end of the local market rates.

D. HOW IS A NON-PROFIT CO-OP FINANCED?

Housing co-operatives obtain their mortgages from private financial institutions. CMHC insures the lender against payment default; in addition, it provides operating subsidies to make the co-operative affordable to moderate- and lower-income households.

1. Federal Co-operative Housing Programs

The federal government introduced major co-operative housing programs in 1973, 1978, and 1986. Approximately 55,000 units of co-operative housing have been funded through a variety of programs, including some provincial programs. The programs aided the development of co-operative housing through insuring private sector mortgages and providing assistance to reduce housing charges to market rent levels.

The current federal program is based on an innovative index-linked mortgage (ILM). With the ILM, the interest rate is linked to the annual rate of inflation expected over the entire life of the mortgage. Payments are therefore lower than those on regular mortgages in the early years of the project. However, over the long term they even out with regular mortgages. The central features of the current federal program are as follows:

- Thirty-year private sector loans to cover up to 100% of project costs, with an extension to 35 years possible if a co-op needs to defer payments
- Federal annual assistance to bring housing charges down to local market rent levels in the year the co-op opens
- Assistance for new construction and renovations
- Five thousand dollars per unit to assist with adaptation of 5% of units in a co-op for the physically disabled, where practical
- Requirements that a minimum of 15% and a maximum of 50% of each co-operative's units be occupied by low-income households receiving low rent supplements (supplements are cost-shared by the federal and provincial governments)
- Internal security of tenure fund established by the co-operative to assist members facing affordability problems after they move in
- Internal replacement reserve fund for maintenance or replacement of major capital items such as roofs and appliances
- ILM stabilization fund to assist ILM co-ops with financial problems

2. Provincial Co-operative Housing Programs

The provinces of Quebec, Ontario, and Manitoba have been particularly active in the field of assisting non-profit housing. Their programs, and programs of other provinces, are constantly changing.

(a) Quebec
Quebec has been a leader among provinces in funding housing co-operatives. Between 1984 and 1986 Quebec sponsored a program which extended assistance to private and non-profit landlords for the renovation or conversion of existing buildings and the construction of new units. Presently Quebec is involved with a federal/provincial cost-shared non-profit housing program. This involves a cost-shared rent supplement assistance for 100% of units to ensure qualifying households pay no more than 25% of income for housing.

(b) Ontario
Ontario's co-operative housing program was introduced in 1986 and the costs are shared by the federal and provincial governments. Its features include:

- Government-insured private market financing
- The requirement that a minimum of 40% of units in co-operatives be occupied by households receiving rent supplements
- Annual assistance to bring initial housing charges down to the level of local market rents, with this assistance being gradually withdrawn over a period of years
- The requirement that 25% of units be reserved for households falling into the "neediest" category as defined by the province, with the re-

maining 15% reserved for "core-need" households as defined by the federal government

- Allowance for individual co-operatives to exceed the 40% minimum described above and to subsidize households that, while not in "core" need, are unable to afford the housing charge without spending more than 25% of gross income
- A focus on new construction, though some assistance is available for rehabilitation of existing housing

(c) Manitoba

Manitoba's co-operative home-start program was introduced in 1986 to enable co-operative groups to renovate or convert existing (pre-1961) buildings to housing co-operatives. The main features of the program are as follows:

- Direct government loans that reduce interest rates to finance up to 100% of eligible project costs
- Additional assistance to reduce housing charges to the lower range of local market rent levels
- Development funding and start-up assistance for feasibility studies to carry the project to the stage of design and cost estimate
- Rent supplement assistance to reduce rents to 25% of income for qualifying households
- Requirements that a minimum of 5% of units per project must incorporate design features to enable easy adaptation for physically disabled co-operative members
- Additional assistance available to projects which develop units accessible to and adapted for the disabled

The Manitoba government also provides additional rent supplement funding through its complementary assistance program. This funding is targetted to households that are not eligible under ILM program guidelines for rent supplement assistance, but whose incomes are too low to enable them to pay market housing charges without exceeding the federal/provincial income guideline of 30%.

E. ADVANTAGES AND DISADVANTAGES OF NON-PROFIT CO-OP HOUSING

1. Advantages

- Members of housing co-ops have the right to permanent residency as long as they respect the obligations of membership and adhere to the by-laws and rules and regulations. Joint ownership eliminates the insecurity of the rental market by putting control of the housing units in the hands of resident members.

- You pay lower-than-market rent and the initial cash purchase for your shares in the co-op is minimal.
- Rather than rent being based on market demand, it is related only to any additional costs that are incurred by the co-operative for operational or other purposes.
- If there is any excess of earnings over expenditures, this can be passed on to members by means of a reduction in monthly rent payments.
- Housing is available on a non-profit basis. Co-operative housing is designed to be affordable, and it may not be bought or sold for profit.
- There is democratic control by members: each member has one vote in decision-making on important matters such as the election of directors, housing charges, and the rules and regulations members are required to follow.
- Because of the co-operative nature of this type of housing, members may feel a unique sense of community that they would not feel in a rental apartment.
- Members may share similar philosophies relating to the co-operative concept.
- Within the budget limits set by members, the co-ops attempt to provide the highest-quality housing possible, both in initial construction and through continuing maintenance. Government assistance mortgage financing ensures that capital reserves exist to fund the replacement of worn-out buildings and equipment.
- The membership in co-ops is open to anyone who meets the eligibility requirement.
- Government subsidies can lower housing costs.
- There are no resale or sub-letting problems if you must move for any reason. You receive your initial share purchase funds back.
- You can obtain a larger or smaller unit if your family situation changes, yet you remain in the same community.

2. Disadvantages

- There is no return on your initial investment of share equity in the co-operative. The original amount paid into the co-operative is returned, so no capital gains are possible.
- The requirement to actively participate in the co-operative by attending committee meetings and/or assisting in the general maintenance of the co-op may not be compatible with your needs or desire for autonomy.
- The waiting time to get into a co-operative may be substantial.

•   The selection of co-operatives available may not be suitable for your lifestyle needs. For example, if you are retired, you may not want to be in a community with a large percentage of young families with children.

F. HOW DO PEOPLE BECOME NON-PROFIT CO-OP MEMBERS?

There are several ways that you can initiate the process of exploring the co-op option. You can contact local co-op housing federations or resource groups. You may wish to join as a member of a developing co-op, or make a direct application to an existing co-op.

See Sample 7, a common co-operative housing application form. Most existing co-ops close their waiting lists once they have reached a certain number, but potential members are still interviewed, and are contacted when space becomes available. As mentioned earlier, you can find the names of co-operatives by looking in the Yellow Pages. A list of the housing federations in Canada is contained in Appendix A.

SAMPLES

SAMPLE 1
(Chapter 3)

Operating Budget

ABC Condominium Corporation
Proposed 1989 Operating Budget

Income:

Laundry machines	$ 7,600
Parking	8,500
Operating assessments	339,054
Recreation centre fees	500
Late charges	500
Interest	4,100
Rental	7,300
Antenna lease	10,000
TOTAL INCOME	$377,554

Expenditures, general:

Audit	$ 1,500
Bank charges	400
Duplicating/postage	2,100
General meeting	350
Insurance	11,200
Legal	1,100
Management fees	24,100
Miscellaneous	600
Real estate taxes	2,250
Wages, caretaker	50,100
Wages, casual	3,100
Wages, security	600
TOTAL GENERAL EXPENDITURES	$ 97,400

Expenditures, building:

Boiler and mechanical	$ 15,100
Electricity	56,600
Elevator/licences	14,700
Emergency generator	1,000
Extermination	1,200
Fire protection equipment	3,100
Garage door	700
General maintenance	2,300
Heating/fuel	98,100
Laundry equipment	1,100
Painting	1,100
Refuse removal	2,665
Repairs, exterior	5,600
Repairs, interior	3,100

Supplies	2,100
Telephone/pager/enterphone	1,900
Window cleaning	1,600
TOTAL BUILDING EXPENDITURES	$211,965

Expenditures, grounds:

Landscaping	$ 10,100
Repairs	1,100
Roadway/sewer maintenance	800
Supplies	350
TOTAL GROUNDS EXPENDITURES	$ 12,350

Expenditures, recreation facilities:

Repairs	$ 5,100
Supplies	1,200
TOTAL RECREATION EXPENDITURES	$ 6,300

Expenditures, debt-service:

Caretaker suite lead	$ 2,980
First mortgage	24,100
Satellite repairs	1,100
TOTAL DEBT-SERVICE EXPENDITURES	$ 28,180

TOTAL EXPENDITURES	$356,195
Reserves: Contingency fund	$ 21,359
TOTAL ALL EXPENDITURES AND RESERVES	$377,554

SAMPLE 2
(Chapter 2)

Set of Financial Statements

**The Owners, ABC Condominium Corporation
Financial Statements**

December 31, 1988

Contents

Auditor's Report
Notes to Financial Statements

Auditor's Report

February 12, 1989

To the Owners
ABC Condominium Corporation

I have examined the balance sheet of the ABC Condominium Corporation as at December 31, 1988 and the statements of income, expenditures, and maintenance reserve fund surplus for the year then ended. My examination was made in accordance with generally accepted auditing standards, and accordingly included such tests and other procedures as I considered necessary in the circumstances.

In my opinion, these financial statements present fairly the financial position of the Condominium Corporation as at December 31, 1988 and the results of its operations for the year then ended in accordance with generally accepted accounting principles applied on a basis consistent with that of the preceding year.

R. Martin
Chartered Accountant

STATEMENT I

**The Owners, ABC Condominium Corporation
Balance Sheet**

December 31, 1988

	1988	1987
ASSETS		
Current assets:		
Cash, operating fund	$ 7,971	$ 1,907
Cash, maintenance reserve fund	50,232	2,045
Term deposits, maintenance reserve fund	—	40,000
Accounts receivable	4,299	2,195
Prepaid expenses	—	9,779
	62,502	55,926
Fixed assets, at cost:		
Caretaker suites (Note 3)	202,410	202,410
TOTAL ASSETS	$264,912	$258,336
LIABILITIES		
Current liabilities:		
Accounts payable and accrued	$ 1,200	$ 43,832
Current portion of long-term debt	2,741	1,375
	3,941	45,207
Long-term debt:		
Mortgages payable (Note 4)	$188,192	$190,933
OWNERS' EQUITY (DEFICIT)		
Surplus (deficit) (Note 6):		
Operating fund:		
Balance at beginning of year	$ (12,660)	$ (5,280)
Deficit recovery, special assessment (Note 8)	12,660	—
Appropriated from (to) maintenance reserve fund	12,700	(7,380)
	12,700	(12,660)
Maintenance reserve fund:		
Statement II	60,079	34,856
	72,779	22,196
TOTAL LIABILITIES AND EQUITY (DEFICIT)	$264,912	$258,336

Approved by the Condominium Council:

_____ , Council Member

_____ , Council Member

The Owners, ABC Condominium Corporation
Statement of Maintenance Reserve Fund Surplus

Year Ended December 31, 1988

	1988		1987
	Budget	Actual	Actual
Balance at beginning of year	$34,856	$34,856	$87,977
Special assessment	—	—	12,800
Excess of income over expenditures for the year, Statement III	25,223	37,923	(3,801)
	60,079	72,779	96,976
Appropriations from reserve fund:			
Appropriated from (to) operating fund surplus	—	(12,700)	7,380
Energy conservation	—	—	(6,700)
Waterproofing	—	—	(62,800)
	—	(12,700)	(62,120)
Balance at end of year (Note 6)	$60,079	$60,079	$34,856

Represented by:	1988	1987
Maintenance reserve fund:		
Cash	$50,232	$ 2,045
Term deposits	—	40,000
	50,232	42,045
Operating fund:		
Net assets	9,847	(7,189)
	$60,079	$34,856

The Owners, ABC Condominium Corporation
Statement of Income and Expenditures

Year Ended December 31, 1988

	1988		1987
	Budget	Actual	Actual
Income:			
Special assessments (Note 8)	$ 14,400	$ 4,264	$ —
Assessments	335,692	335,557	313,471
Interest and other......................................	10,560	13,973	18,799
Coin laundry..	10,680	5,865	8,653
Parking..	8,200	8,225	9,735
Caretaker suites' rental	5,700	4,818	5,150
	385,252	382,702	355,808

Expenditures (Statement IV):

General	119,262	127,526	115,926
Building	234,800	208,597	230,538
Grounds	3,267	6,614	9,743
Recreational facilities	2,700	2,042	3,402
	360,029	344,779	359,609

Excess of income over expenditures
for the year .... $ 25,223 $ 37,923 $ (3,801)

STATEMENT IV

The Owners, ABC Condominium Corporation
Statement of Expenditures

Year Ended December 31, 1988

OPERATING FUND

	1988 Budget	1988 Actual	1987 Actual
General expenses:			
Staff	$ 49,884	$ 49,875	$ 51,042
Insurance	14,958	11,279	9,897
Management fees	24,300	24,100	22,950
Professional fees (Note 8)	—	6,629	1,217
Sundry	2,400	9,695	4,892
Property tax assessment, caretaker suites, etc.	27,720	25,948	25,928
	119,262	127,526	115,926
Building:			
Electricity and heating	171,916	143,601	133,260
General maintenance	22,372	22,525	21,177
Repairs	20,592	24,286	32,487
Scavenging	2,424	1,710	1,944
Waterproofing	—	—	10,373
Enterphone, pager, and telephone	2,700	2,830	10,778
Energy conservation	—	—	6,475
Elevator	14,796	13,645	14,044
	234,800	208,597	230,538
Grounds:			
Maintenance and supplies	3,267	6,614	9,743
Recreational facilities:			
Pool supplies and repairs	2,700	2,042	3,402
	$360,029	$344,779	$359,609

The Owners, ABC Condominium Corporation
Notes to Financial Statements

December 31, 1988

1. ACCOUNTING POLICIES

Capital Expenditures

Assets of an enduring nature, other than the caretaker suites (Note 3), are expensed in the year acquired.

Maintenance Reserve Fund

Pursuant to various sections of the provincial Condominium Act, the Condominium Corporation is required to establish a Maintenance Reserve Fund to provide resources to pay unusual or extraordinary non-annual expenditures such as the repair, maintenance, and replacement of common property. A levy thereto of not less than 5% of the Condominium Corporation's annual budget is required until the reserve fund represents at least 25% of its total annual budget.

2. OPERATIONS

The Condominium Corporation has been established under the provisions of the provincial Condominium Act for the purpose of the control, management, and administration of the common property, facilities, and assets of the corporation.

3. CARETAKER SUITES

The caretaker suites have been recorded in the accounts at original cost. The corporation has adopted a policy of not providing for depreciation on, nor recognizing changes in the market value of, the suites.

	1988	1987
Suite #101	$100,800	$100,800
Suite #202	101,610	101,610
	$202,410	$202,410

4. LONG-TERM DEBT

Mortgages Payable, MPS Development Corporation

Condo Lot	Monthly Payment	Interest Rate	Total	Current Portion	1988	1987
86	$980.87	11.0%	$ 95,190	$1,367	$ 93,823	$ 95,190
262	986.46	11.0%	95,743	1,374	94,369	95,743
			$190,933	$2,741	$188,192	$190,933

The mortgages are secured by the caretaker suites.

5. INCOME TAXES

The income of the Condominium Corporation is derived substantially from member sources, and as such, is viewed by Revenue Canada as a reduction of member contributions and not income of the corporation. Accordingly, no provision for income taxes is recorded in the accompanying financial statements.

6. SURPLUS

Notwithstanding the statutory maintenance reserve fund requirements referred to in Note 1 above, the Condominium Corporation has determined that a maintenance reserve fund of

$60,079 be established at December 31, 1988 to meet its anticipated future maintenance requirements. At the financial statement date, surplus funds amounting to $60,079 have been accumulated for this purpose, which represents 100% of the budgeted reserve. Surplus in excess of such reserve requirements is set out in Statement I as Operating Fund Surplus.

7. COMPARATIVE FIGURES

The prior year's comparative figures are based upon financial statements which were reported on by other auditors. Certain prior years' comparative figures have been restated to conform to the presentation adopted for 1988.

8. SPECIAL ASSESSMENTS

During the year the corporation levied special assessments for the purposes outlined below:

	Assessment Levied
Funds to cover 1988 under-budgeted expenses	$ 6,400
Satellite repairs	3,500
Arbitration costs	4,500
Total, Statement III	14,400
Operating deficit recovery, Statement I	12,660
	$27,060

The cost of satellite repairs paid in 1988 totalled $3,874 and is included in Building: General maintenance (Statement IV).

Arbitration costs amounting to $4,500 were paid in 1988 and are included in General Expenses: Professional fees (Statement IV).

SAMPLE 3
(Chapter 3)

Personal Cost of Living Budget (Monthly)

A. Income (Average monthly income, actual or estimated)

Salary, bonuses, and commissions ....$ _____
Dividends ....$ _____
Interest income ....$ _____
Pension income ....$ _____
Other:

_____ $ _____
_____ $ _____

TOTAL MONTHLY INCOME ....$ _____

B. Expenses

Regular monthly payments:
Rent or mortgage payments ....$ _____
Automobile(s) ....$ _____
Appliances/TV ....$ _____
Home improvement loan ....$ _____
Credit card payments (not covered elsewhere) ....$ _____

Personal loan ....$ _____
Medical plan ....$ _____
Installment and other loans ....$ _____
Life insurance premiums ....$ _____
House insurance ....$ _____
Other insurance premiums (auto, extended medical, etc.) .. $ _____
RRSP deductions ....$ _____
Pension fund (employer) ....$ _____
Investment plan(s) ....$ _____
Other:

_____ $ _____
_____ $ _____
Miscellaneous ....$ _____
    TOTAL REGULAR MONTHLY PAYMENTS ....$ _____

Household operating expenses:
Telephone ....$ _____
Gas and electricity ....$ _____
Heat ....$ _____
Water and garbage ....$ _____
Other household expenses (repairs, maintenance, etc.) .....$ _____
Other:

_____ $ _____
_____ $ _____
    TOTAL HOUSEHOLD OPERATING EXPENSES ....$ _____

Food expenses:
At home ....$ _____
Away from home ....$ _____
    TOTAL FOOD EXPENSES ....$ _____

Personal expenses
Clothing, cleaning, laundry ....$ _____
Drugs ....$ _____
Transportation (other than auto) ....$ _____
Medical/dental ....$ _____
Day care ....$ _____
Education (self) ....$ _____
Education (children) ....$ _____
Dues ....$ _____
Gifts, donations, and dues ....$ _____
Travel ....$ _____
Recreation ....$ _____
Newspapers, magazines, books ....$ _____
Automobile maintenance, gas, and parking ....$ _____
Spending money, allowances ....$ _____
Other:

_____ $ _____
_____ $ _____
    TOTAL PERSONAL EXPENSES ....$ _____

Tax expenses:

    Federal and provincial income taxes ....$ _____

    Home property taxes ....$ _____

    Other:

    _____$ _____

    TOTAL TAX EXPENSES ....$ _____

C. Summary of Expenses

Regular monthly payments ....$ _____

Household operating expenses ....$ _____

Food expenses ....$ _____

Personal expenses ....$ _____

Tax expenses ....$ _____

    TOTAL MONTHLY EXPENSES ....$ _____

    TOTAL MONTHLY DISPOSABLE INCOME

    AVAILABLE (Subtract total monthly expenses from total

    monthly income) ....$ _____

SAMPLE 4
(Chapter 3)

Calculating Your Gross Debt Service (GDS) Ratio

Your GDS Ratio is calculated by adding the total of your monthly mortgage principal, interest, and taxes (PIT) together and dividing that figure by your monthly income. Guidelines have been set that allow a maximum of 27% to 30%, depending on the financial institution, of your gross income to be used for the mortgage PIT.

$$\text{GDS Ratio} = \frac{\text{Monthly principal} + \text{Interest} + \text{Taxes (PIT)}}{\text{Monthly income}}$$

Gross (pre-tax) **monthly** income of purchaser(s) ....$ _____

Other forms of income (e.g., annual) averaged to monthly ......$ _____

    TOTAL MONTHLY INCOME ....$ _____

Estimate **monthly** property tax on home (net after any

provincial homeowners' grant is taken into consideration,

if applicable) ....$ _____

1. To estimate the **maximum** monthly mortgage payment **plus** property taxes you could carry (monthly PIT), calculate 30% of the total monthly income:

    30% of $ _____$ _____

2. To estimate the **maximum** monthly mortgage payment, not including taxes (PI), that you could carry, subtract the monthly tax amount from the monthly PIT:

    Monthly PIT ....$ _____

Less: Monthly property tax .... $ _____
MAXIMUM MONTHLY MORTGAGE PAYMENT
(not including taxes) = Monthly PI .... $ _____

Use Chart 4 to determine the maximum mortgage (not including taxes) for which you qualify under your GDS Ratio guidelines. Simply look up your maximum monthly mortgage payment under the current interest rate.

Maximum mortgage available under GDS Ratio guidelines = $ _____

SAMPLE 5
(Chapter 3)

Calculation of Total Debt Service (TDS) Ratio

Most lenders require that an applicant meet a TDS Ratio, in addition to looking at the GDS Ratio. The TDS Ratio is a maximum of 35% to 40% of gross income—actual rules may vary between financial institutions. The TDS Ratio is calculated in much the same way as the GDS Ratio, but takes into consideration all other debts and loans you may have.

$$\text{TDS Ratio} = \frac{\text{Monthly principal + Interest + Taxes (PIT) + Other monthly payments}}{\text{Monthly income}}$$

Gross (pre-tax) **monthly** income of purchaser(s) .... $ _____
Other forms of income (e.g., annual) averaged to monthly .... $ _____
TOTAL MONTHLY INCOME .... $ _____

Other monthly payments:
Credit cards .... $ _____
Other mortgages .... $ _____
Car loan .... $ _____
Other loans .... $ _____
Alimony/child support .... $ _____
Charge accounts .... $ _____
Other debts (list):

_____ $ _____
_____ $ _____
_____ $ _____
_____ $ _____
TOTAL OTHER MONTHLY PAYMENTS .... $ _____

To calculate your TDS Ratio, take 40% of $_____ (total monthly income) = $_____ available for Monthly principal + Interest + Taxes + Other payments (PIT + Other).

To estimate the **maximum monthly mortgage payment** you could carry within your allowable TDS Ratio:

Monthly PIT + Other ....$ _____
Less: Other monthly payments ....$ _____
SUBTOTAL ....$ _____
Less: Estimated property taxes ....$ _____
MAXIMUM MONTHLY MORTGAGE PAYMENT ....$ _____

Use Chart 4 to determine the maximum mortgage for which you qualify under the
TDS Ratio guidelines. Simply look up your maximum monthly mortgage payment
under the current interest rate.

Maximum mortgage available under TDS Ratio guidelines = $ _____

SAMPLE 6
(Chapter 3)

Mortgage Application Form

Status of Applicant: Purchaser _____   Present Owner ____
Name: _____ Social Ins.: _____
    Mr./Mrs./Miss/Ms. First Surname

Address: _____ How Long? _____

_____

Type of	___ First	___ Fixed Rate	___ NHA
Mortgage	___ Second	___ Adjustable Rate	___ Conventional
Required:	___ Weekly	___ Monthly	___ Insured
	___ Biweekly	___ Semimonthly	

$ _____ Amount   _____ Term (years and months)
% _____ Interest Rate   _____ Amortization Period (years)
       Monthly Payment   _____ Date Funds Required
$ _____ (include taxes)
Name of
Applicant's Lawyer: _____ Telephone: _____
Address of Lawyer: _____
Purpose of Loan: _____
If Purchase: $ _____ Purchase Price $ _____ Cash Down Payment
          $ _____ Other Financing
If Refinancing $ _____ Present Mtge. Balance _____ Present Lender
Existing Loan: _____ Maturity Date _____ Reference No.
For Inspection of Property, Contact:

_____Telephone: _____
Application Submitted By:
_____Telephone: _____
Description of Property to Be Mortgaged
Full Address: _____
Lot Size ___ x ___ $ ___ Annual Taxes $_____ Annual Maintenance Fee
Lot Number _____   ____ Plan No. _____Township
Building To Be Occupied by Applicant? _____

Building To Be Rented Out? _____ $_____ Annual Rental Income
Description: ____ Detached   ____ Triplex   ____ Condominium
                ____ Semi-detached   ____ Row   ____ Other (specify)
Have the buildings ever been insulated with urea
formaldehyde foam insulation?   Yes_____   No _____

Personal Information
Previous Address (if less than three years at present address):
_____
Spouse's Full Name: _____
Home Telephone: _____ Business Telephone: _____
Date of Birth: _____ Number of Dependents: _____
Name of Employer: _____
Occupation: _____ Years of Service: _____
Previous Employer: _____
Occupation: _____ Years of Service: _____
Annual Income: $ _____   Basic $ _____   Other (specify)
                  $ _____   Commissions $ _____   TOTAL

Complete this section if there is a co-applicant or guarantor. (If the person is
other than the spouse of the applicant, a separate application is required.)
Co-applicant: _____   Guarantor: _____
Name: _____ Social Ins.:_____
        Mr./Mrs./Miss/Ms.   First   Surname
Address:_____
_____
Previous address (if less than three years at present address):
_____
Spouse's Full Name: _____
Home Telephone: _____ Business Telephone: _____
Date of Birth: _____ Number of Dependents: _____
Name of Employer: _____
Occupation: _____ Years of Service: _____
Previous Employer: _____
Occupation: _____ Years of Service: _____
Annual Income: $ _____   Basic $_____   Other (specify)
                  $ _____   Commissions $_____   TOTAL

Personal Financial Information
Assets
Residence $ _____
Cash on deposit (give name(s) & address(es) $ _____
of trust company or bank) $ _____
Automobile (year & make) $ _____
Other real estate (give address(es)) $ _____
Term deposits (give name & address of bank) $ _____
Stocks/bonds (give total market value) $ _____
RRSPs (give name & address of broker) $ _____
Other assets (give description of each) $ _____
    TOTAL ASSETS $_____

Liabilities	Balance Owing	Monthly Payments
Existing mortgages on residence (give name & address of lender)	$ _____	$ _____
Other loans (give name(s) & address(es) of financial institutions)	$ _____	$ _____
Automobile loans (give name & address of lender)	$ _____	$ _____
Other mortgages (give name & address of lender)	$ _____	$ _____
Credit cards (give whom issued by and account number)	$ _____	$ _____
Other liabilities (give description)	$ _____	$ _____
TOTAL LIABILITIES	$ _____	$ _____

NET WORTH (total assets minus total liabilities): $ _____

Please read and sign below.

Financial Institution: _____ Branch Address: _____

Name(s) of Account Holder(s)_____ Account Number: _____

I certify that the above is true and complete and I will provide confirmation if required. You may use any source for information related to this application and each source is authorized to provide you with this confidential information. If requested you are authorized to provide credit information to other credit grantors, consumer reporting agencies, and credit bureaus.

_____
Applicant's Signature

_____
Date

_____
Co-Applicant's Signature

_____
Guarantor's Signature
(if not a co-applicant)

SAMPLE 7
(Chapter 5)

Co-operative Housing Application Form

Forwarded To: _____
Name of Co-op

Name: _____ _____
      Last   First   Date of Birth

Phone: _____ _____ _____
       Home   Work   Other

Address: _____
Suite Number, Street Address

_____ _____
City/Province   Postal Code

List all other persons who will be residing with you:

Name	Sex	Date of Birth (d/m/y)
_____	_____	_____
_____	_____	_____
_____	_____	_____
_____	_____	_____

Number of Bedrooms Required (circle one only):   1   2   3   4
(You may have no less than one person per bedroom and no more than two persons per bedroom.)

Special Needs or Requirements (e.g., physical): _____
_____

Number of Vehicles: _____

Pets? (If so, how many and what kind?) _____

Have you ever previously resided in a housing co-operative? Yes ____ No ____

If so, where and when? _____

Current Housing: _____   _____   _____   _____
                    Own   Rent   Co-op   Other (specify)

List last two places you have lived:

Address	How Long?	Name of Landlord	Phone No.
_____	_____	_____	_____
_____	_____	_____	_____

List two personal references (other than family):

Name	Address	Phone No.
_____	_____	_____
_____	_____	_____

According to the structure of co-operative living and the lease that you will sign before you move in, you will be expected to attend the general meetings and contribute to the successful running of the co-operative by attending committee meetings and/or assisting in the general maintenance of the co-op.

Please indicate your hobbies and/or skills or areas of interest:

Hobbies: _____
_____
_____

Skills:

Accounting	_____	Filing	_____	Music	_____
Artwork	_____	Instructing	_____	Plumbing	_____
Babysitting	_____	Interviewing	_____	Small appliances	_____
Bookkeeping	_____	Janitorial	_____	Typing	_____
Carpentry	_____	Legal	_____	Translation	_____
Computer	_____	Mechanical	_____	Yard work	_____
Electrical	_____	Minutes taking	_____		

Please check which committees you are interested in:

Board	____	Landscaping	____	Newsletter	____
Children's	____	Management	____	Nominating	____
Education	____	Maintenance	____	Security	____
Finance	____	Membership	____	Social	____

Could you assist in, or do you require, language interpretation? If so, in what language?

_____

Annual Income Information

Please list the gross annual income (before taxes) of all family members other than those who are under 19 years of age and in attendance at a recognized educational institution:

Name	Relationship	Annual Amount
_____	_____	_____
_____	_____	_____
_____	_____	_____
_____	_____	_____

TOTAL $ _____

Are you receiving UIC or some other form of assistance? Yes ____ No ____

Please detail the nature of the assistance (government or otherwise), if applicable:

Type of Assistance	Monthly Income
_____	_____
_____	_____

The co-op will require that you fill in a detailed income verification form at a later date.

_____   _____
Signature of Applicant   Date of Application

CHECKLISTS

CHECKLIST 1
(Chapter 1)

Condominium Assessment Checklist

Contents

A. General Information
B. Exterior and Common Elements
C. Interior Common Elements
D. Management
E. Condominium Corporation
F. Recreation
G. Individual Unit
H. Legal and Financial Matters
I. Overall Assessment

Indicate on the line provided your rating of the listed factor as: excellent, good, poor, available, not available, not applicable, etc.

A. General Information
Location of property _____
Condition of neighbourhood _____
Zoning of surrounding areas _____
Prospect for future increase in value _____
Proximity of:
• Schools _____
• Churches _____
• Shopping _____
• Recreation _____
• Entertainment _____
• Parks _____
• Children's playgrounds _____
• Public transportation _____
• Highways _____
• Hospital _____
• Police department _____
• Fire department _____
• Ambulance _____
Traffic density _____
Garbage removal _____
Sewage system _____
Quality of water _____
Taxes:
• Provincial _____
• Municipal _____

Maintenance fees/assessments _____
Easements _____
Quietness of:
• Neighbourhood _____
• Condo complex _____
• Individual unit _____
Percentage of units that are owner-occupied _____
If next to commercial centre, is access to residential
section well controlled? _____
Is adjacent commercial development being planned? _____
Size of development related to your needs
(small, medium, large) _____
Does project seem to be compatible with your lifestyle? _____
Style of development (adult-oriented, children, retirees, etc.) _____
Age of development (new, moderate, old) _____

B. Exterior and Common Elements
Privacy
Roadway (public street, private street, safety for children) _____
Sidewalks (adequacy of drainage) _____
Driveway (public, private, semi-private) _____
Garage:
• Reserved space (one or two cars) _____
• Automatic garage doors _____
• Security _____
• Adequate visitor parking _____
Construction material (brick, wood, stone) _____
Siding (aluminum, other) _____
Condition of paint _____
Roof:
• Type of material _____
• Age _____
• Condition _____
Balcony or patios:
• Location (view, etc.) _____
• Privacy _____
• Size _____
• Open or enclosed _____
Landscaping:
• Trees _____
• Shrubbery, flowers _____
• Lawns _____
• Automatic sprinklering _____
Condition and upkeep of exterior _____

C. Interior Common Elements
Intercom system _____
Medical alert system _____

Fire safety system (fire alarms, smoke detectors)   _____
Burglar alarm system   _____
General safety:
- TV surveillance   _____
- Controlled access   _____
Pre-wired for television and telephone cable   _____
Lobby:
- Cleanliness   _____
- Decor   _____
- Doorman   _____
Public corridors:
- Material used   _____
- Condition   _____
- Plaster (free of cracks, stains)   _____
- Decor   _____
Stairs:
- General accessibility   _____
- Number of stairwells   _____
Elevators   _____
Wheelchair accessibility   _____
Storage facilities:
- Location   _____
- Size   _____
Insulation:
(The R factor is the measure of heating and cooling efficiency. The higher the R factor, the more efficient.)
- R rating in walls (minimum of R-19; depends on geographic location)   _____
- R rating in ceiling (minimum of R-30; depends on geographic location)   _____
- Heat pumps   _____
- Windows (insulated, storm, screen)   _____
Temperature controls:
- Individually controlled   _____
- Convenient location   _____
Plumbing:
- Functions well   _____
- Convenient fixtures   _____
- Quietness of plumbing   _____
Suitable water pressure   _____
Heating and air conditioning (gas, electric, hot water, oil)   _____
Utility costs:
- Gas   _____
- Electric   _____
- Other   _____
Laundry facilities   _____
Soundproofing features   _____

D. Management

Condominium management company

Owner-managed (condominium council/board of directors)   _____

Resident manager   _____

Management personnel:

- Front desk   _____
- Maintenance   _____
- Gardener   _____
- Trash removal   _____
- Snow removal   _____
- Security (number of guards, hours, location, patrol)   _____

E. Condominium Corporation

Activity of corporation   _____

Average age of other owners   _____

F. Recreation

Clubhouse   _____

Club membership fees (included, not included)   _____

Sports:

- Courts (tennis, squash, racquetball, handball, basketball)   _____
- Games room (ping pong, billiards)   _____
- Exercise room   _____
- Bicycle path/jogging track   _____
- Organized sports and activities   _____

Children's playground:

- Location (accessibility)   _____
- Noise factor   _____
- Organized sports and activities (supervised)   _____

Swimming pool:

- Location (outdoor, indoor)   _____
- Children's pool   _____
- Noise factor   _____

Visitors' accommodation   _____

G. Individual Unit

Location in complex   _____

Size of unit   _____

Is the floor plan and layout suitable?   _____

Will your furnishings fit in?   _____

Is the unit exposed to the sunlight?   _____

Does the unit have a scenic view?   _____

Is the unit in a quiet location (away from garbage unit,
elevator noise, playgrounds, etc.)?   _____

Accessibility (stairs, elevators, fire exits)   _____

Closets:

- Number   _____
- Location   _____

Carpet:
- Colour   _____
- Quality/texture _____

Hardwood floors   _____

Living room:
- Size/shape   _____
- Windows/view   _____
- Sunlight (morning, afternoon) _____
- Fireplace   _____
- Privacy (from outside, from rest of condo) _____

Dining room:
- Size   _____
- Accessibility to kitchen _____
- Windows/view   _____

Den or family room:
- Size/shape   _____
- Windows/view (morning or afternoon sunlight) _____
- Fireplace   _____
- Privacy (from outside, from rest of condo) _____

Laundry room:
- Work space available _____
- Washer and dryer _____
- Size/capacity   _____
- Warranty coverage _____

Kitchen:
- Size   _____
- Eating facility (table, nook, no seating) _____
- Floors (linoleum, tile, wood) _____
- Exhaust system _____
- Counter top built in _____
- Counter top material (warranty coverage?) _____
- Work space   _____
- Kitchen cabinets (number, accessibility) _____
- Cabinet material (warranty coverage?) _____
- Sink (size, single, double) _____
- Sink material   _____
- Built-in cutting boards _____
- Oven (single, double, self-cleaning) _____
- Gas or electric oven _____
- Age of oven (warranty coverage?) _____
- Microwave (size) _____
- Age of microwave (warranty coverage?) _____
- Refrigerator/freezer (size, capacity) _____
- Refrigerator (frost-free, icemaker, single/double door) _____
- Age of refrigerator (warranty coverage?) _____
- Dishwasher (age; warranty coverage?) _____
- Trash compactor/garbage disposal (warranty coverage?) _____

- Pantry or storage area   _____
Number of bedrooms   _____
Master bedroom:
- Size/shape   _____
- Privacy (from outside, from rest of condo)   _____
- Closets/storage space   _____
- Fireplace   _____
- Floor and wall covering   _____
Master bathroom (en suite):
- Size   _____
- Bathtub   _____
- Whirlpool tub   _____
- Shower   _____
- Steam room   _____
- Vanity   _____
- Sink (single, double, integrated sink bowls)   _____
- Medicine cabinet   _____
Number of bathrooms   _____
Complete, or sink and toilet only?   _____
Overall condition of condo   _____
Overall appearance and decor of condo   _____

H. Legal and Financial Matters

Project documents (e.g., disclosure/declaration) received
and read   _____
By-laws received and read   _____
Rules and regulations received and read   _____
Financial statements received and read   _____
Estoppel certificate received and read   _____
Other documents (list):

_____
_____
_____
_____

All above documentation (as applicable) reviewed by
your lawyer   _____
Financial statements reviewed by your accountant or
independent condominium management company   _____
All assessments, maintenance fees, and taxes detailed   _____
Condominium corporation insurance coverage adequate   _____
Restrictions acceptable (e.g., pets, renting out unit,
number of people living in suite, children, etc.)   _____
Condominium unit insurance package estimate obtained   _____
All verbal promises or representations of sales representative
agent, or broker written into the offer to purchase   _____
Other:

_____
_____

I. Overall Assessment

_____

_____

_____

CHECKLIST 2
(Chapter 2)

Condominium Purchase Expenses

In addition to the actual purchase price of your home, there are a number of other expenses to be paid on or prior to closing. Not all of these expenses will be applicable.

Type of Expense	When Paid	Estimated Amount
Deposit	At time of offer	_____
Mortgage application fee	At time of application	_____
Property appraisal	At time of mortgage application	_____
Property inspection	At inspection	_____
Balance of purchase price	On closing	_____
Legal fees re property transfer	On closing	_____
Legal fees re mortgage preparation	On closing	_____
Legal disbursements re property transfer	On closing	_____
Legal disbursements re mortgage preparation	On closing	_____
Mortgage broker commission	On closing	_____
Property survey	On closing	_____
Property tax holdback	On closing	_____
Land transfer or deed tax	On closing	_____
Property purchase tax	On closing	_____
Property tax adjustment	On closing	_____
New Home Warranty Program fee	On closing	_____
Mortgage interest adjustment	On closing	_____
Sales tax on chattels purchased from vendor	On closing	_____
Adjustments for fuel, taxes, etc.	On closing	_____
Mortgage lender insurance (CMHC or MICC premium)	On closing	_____
Condominium reserve fund advance	On closing	_____
Home and property insurance	On closing	_____
Life insurance premium on amount of outstanding mortgage	On closing	_____
Moving expenses	At time of move	_____
Utility connection charges	At time of move	_____
Home and garden implements	Shortly after purchase	_____
Redecorating and refurbishing costs	Shortly after purchase	_____
Immediate repair and maintenance costs	Shortly after purchase	_____

Other expenses (list):

<table>
<tr><td>_____</td><td>_____</td></tr>
<tr><td>_____</td><td>_____</td></tr>
<tr><td>_____</td><td>_____</td></tr>
</table>

TOTAL CASH REQUIRED ....$_____

CHECKLIST 3
(Chapter 3)

Mortgage Checklist

A. Ask Yourself These Questions

1. Is your income secure? _____

2. Will your income increase or decrease in the future? _____

3. Are you planning on increasing the size of your family (e.g., children, relatives) and therefore your living expenses? _____

4. Will you be able to put aside a financial buffer for unexpected expenses or emergencies? _____

5. Are you planning to purchase the house with someone else? _____

6. If the answer is yes to the above question, will you be able to depend on your partner's financial contribution without interruption? _____

7. If you are relying on an income from renting out all or part of your condominium, have you determined:
   - If city by-laws permit it? _____
   - If the condominium corporation by-laws permit it? _____
   - If the mortgage company policies permit it? _____

8. Have you thoroughly compared mortgage rates and features so that you know what type of mortgage and mortgage company you want? _____

9. Have you determined the amount of mortgage that you would be eligible for? _____

10. Have you considered the benefits of a pre-approved mortgage? _____

11. Have you considered talking to a mortgage broker? _____

12. Have you considered assuming an existing mortgage? _____

13. Have you considered having the vendor give you a mortgage? _____

14. Have you determined all the expenses you will incur relating to the mortgage transaction? (See Checklist 2.) _____

15. Have you completed your present and projected financial needs analysis (income and expenses)? (See Sample 1.) _____

16. Have you completed the mortgage application form, including net worth statement (assets and liabilities)? (See Sample 6.) _____

B. Ask the Lender These Questions

Interest Rates

17. What is the current interest rate (generally, based on the mortgage terms)?

18. How frequently is the interest calculated? (Semiannually? Monthly? Etc.) _____

19. How long will the lender guarantee a quoted interest rate? _____

20. Will the lender put the above guarantee in writing? _____

21. Will you receive a lower rate of interest if the rates fall before you finalize your mortgage?

22. Will the lender put the above reduction assurance in writing? _____

23. Will the lender show you the total amount of interest you will have to pay over the lifetime of the mortgage? _____

Amortization

24. What options do you have for amortization periods? (10 years? 15 years? Etc.) _____

25. Will the lender provide you with an amortization schedule for your loan showing your monthly payments apportioned into principal and interest? _____

26. Have you calculated what your monthly payments will be based on each amortization rate? _____

27. Are you required to maintain the amortized monthly payment schedule if annual prepayments are made, or will they be adjusted accordingly? _____

Term of the Mortgage

28. What different terms are available? (1 year? 2 years? Etc.) _____

29. What is the best term for your personal circumstances? _____

30. What are the different interest rates relating to the terms available? _____

Payments

31. What is the amount of your monthly payments (based on amortization period)? _____

32. Are you permitted to increase the amount of your monthly payments if you want to, without penalty? _____

33. Does the lender have a range of payment periods available, such as weekly, biweekly, monthly, etc.? _____

34. What is the best payment period in your personal circumstances? _____

Prepayment

35. What are your prepayment privileges?
    - Completely open?
    - Open with a fixed penalty or notice requirement? _____
    - Limited open with no penalty or notice requirement? _____
    - Limited open with fixed penalty or notice requirement? _____
    - Completely closed? _____
    - Some combination of the above? _____

36. What amount can be prepaid and what is the penalty or notice required, if applicable? _____
37. How long does the privilege apply in each of the above categories, as applicable? _____
38. When does the prepayment privilege commence? (6 months? 1 year? Etc.) _____
39. Is there a minimum amount that has to be prepaid? _____
40. What form does your prepayment privilege take, increase in payments or lump sum? _____
41. Is your prepayment privilege noncumulative (use it or lose it for that year) or cumulative (e.g., make last year's lump sum prepayment next year)? _____

Taxes

42. How much are the property taxes? _____
43. Does the lender require a property tax payment monthly (based on projected annual tax), or is it optional? _____
44. Does the lender pay interest on the property tax account? If yes, what is the interest rate? _____

Mortgage Transaction Fees and Expenses

45. What is the appraisal fee? Is an appraisal necessary? _____
46. What is the survey fee? Is a survey necessary? _____
47. Will you be able to select a lawyer of your choice to do the mortgage work? _____
48. Does the lender charge a processing or administrative fee? _____
49. Does the lender arrange for a lawyer to do the mortgage documentation work at a flat fee, regardless of the amount of the mortgage? _____
50. Does the lender know what the out-of-pocket disbursements for the mortgage transaction will be? _____
51. Does the mortgage have a renewal administration fee? How much is it? _____

Mortgage Assumption Privileges

52. Can the mortgage be assumed if the property is sold? _____
53. Is the mortgage assumable with or without the lender's approval? _____
54. What are the assumption administrative fees, if any? _____
55. Will the lender release the vendor of all personal obligations under the terms of the mortgage if it is assumed? _____

CHARTS

CHART 1
(Chapter 3)

Amortization Period in Years

The following examples assume a $50,000 mortgage loan and an interest rate* of 13% for the amortization period selected.

Payment	AMORTIZATION PERIOD IN YEARS			
	10	15	20	25
Monthly payment of principal and interest	$ 736.60	$ 621.52	$ 573.77	$ 551.21
Total of mortgage payments over the amortization period	$88,392.00	$111,873.60	$137,702.40	$165,360.00

*Interest being compounded semiannually.

CHART 2
(Chapter 3)

Interest Payments

Interest* on each $1,000 of mortgage is based on payment period.

Interest Rate, %	Weekly, $	Every Two Weeks, $	Twice a Month, $	Monthly, $
8.5	1.82703	3.65698	3.96992	7.95364
9.0	1.90154	3.80629	4.13229	8.27977
9.5	1.97702	3.95756	4.29681	8.61028
10.0	2.05342	4.11069	4.46334	8.94487
10.5	2.13068	4.26555	4.63175	9.28330
11.0	2.20873	4.42201	4.80191	9.62529
11.5	2.28753	4.57996	4.97369	9.97061
12.0	2.36700	4.73930	5.14697	10.31900
12.5	2.44711	4.89991	5.32164	10.67023
13.0	2.52779	5.06169	5.49757	11.02407

*Interest being compounded semiannually.

CHART 3
(Chapter 3)

Prepayment or Increased Payment Savings

Based on a $50,000 mortgage at a 10% interest rate.*

Chart 4 **161**

	Standard Mortgage, 25-Year Amortization	10% Annual Increase in Mortgage Payment	10% Annual Prepayment of Principal
Mortgage repaid in months	300	119	84
Total interest charged	$84,172	$34,449	$20,086
Interest savings vs. standard 25-year mortgage	N/A	$49,723	$64,086

*Interest being compounded semiannually.

CHART 4
(Chapter 3)

Mortgage Amortization Chart

Follow the chart **down,** under the current interest rate, to the amount of your maximum monthly mortgage payment (not including taxes).

Follow that line **to the left** to determine the maximum mortgage, after down payment, for which you may qualify.

Maximum Mortgage*	9%	10%	11%	12%	13%
30,000	248.40	268.50	288.90	309.60	330.90
40,000	341.20	358.00	385.20	412.80	441.20
50,000	414.00	447.50	481.50	516.00	551.50
60,000	496.80	537.00	577.80	619.20	661.80
70,000	579.60	626.50	674.10	722.40	772.10
80,000	662.40	716.00	770.40	825.60	882.40
90,000	745.20	805.50	866.70	928.80	992.70
100,000	828.00	895.00	963.80	1,032.00	1,103.00
110,000	910.80	984.50	1,059.30	1,135.20	1,213.30
120,000	993.60	1,074.00	1,155.60	1,238.40	1,323.60
130,000	1,076.40	1,163.50	1,251.90	1,341.60	1,469.00
140,000	1,159.20	1,253.00	1,348.20	1,444.80	1,544.20
150,000	1,242.00	1,342.50	1,444.50	1,548.00	1,654.50
160,000	1,324.80	1,432.00	1,540.80	1,651.20	1,764.80
170,000	1,407.60	1,521.50	1,637.10	1,754.40	1,875.10
180,000	1,490.40	1,611.00	1,733.40	1,857.60	1,985.40
190,000	1,573.20	1,700.50	1,829.70	1,960.80	2,095.70
200,000	1,656.00	1,790.00	1,926.00	2,064.00	2,206.00

*Based on 25-year amortization period. Amounts are approximate. Interest compounded semiannually.

CHART 5
(Chapter 3)

Monthly Mortgage Payments for Principal plus Interest

The table gives the monthly payment for principal and interest* (not including taxes) for each $1,000 of the amount of the mortgage.

Interest Rate, %	5 Years, $	10 Years, $	15 Years, $	20 Years, $	25 Years, $
8.5	20.44589	12.32023	9.76158	8.58559	7.95364
9.0	20.67873	12.57886	10.04519	8.89190	8.27978
9.5	20.91267	12.83992	10.33227	9.20231	8.61028
10.0	21.14770	13.10337	10.62270	9.51665	8.94488
10.5	21.38381	13.36918	10.91641	9.83474	9.28330
11.0	21.62098	13.63729	11.21327	10.15640	9.62530
11.5	21.85920	13.90767	11.51321	10.48146	9.97061
12.0	22.09846	14.18027	11.81610	10.80975	10.31900
12.5	22.33875	14.45505	12.12186	11.14108	10.67023
13.0	22.58006	14.73197	12.43038	11.47531	11.02408

*Interest being compounded semiannually.

CHART 6
(Chapter 3)

Monthly Income Factors

Interest Rate,* %	Monthly Income Factor	Interest Rate, %	Monthly Income Factor
10	32	15	44
10 1/4	32	15 1/4	44
10 1/2	33	15 1/2	45
10 3/4	34	15 3/4	45
11	34	16	46
11 1/4	35	16 1/4	46
11 1/2	35	16 1/2	47
11 3/4	36	16 3/4	48
12	36	17	48
12 1/4	37	17 1/4	49
12 1/2	38	17 1/2	50
12 3/4	38	17 3/4	50

Chart 7 **163**

13	39		18	51
13 1/4	39		18 1/4	51
13 1/2	40		18 1/2	52
13 3/4	41		18 3/4	53
14	41		19	53
14 1/4	42		19 1/4	54
14 1/2	42		19 1/2	55
14 3/4	43		19 3/4	55
			20	56

*Interest being compounded semiannually.

CHART 7
(Chapter 3)

Monthly Payment Factors

Interest Rate,* %	Monthly Payment Factor	Interest Rate, %	Monthly Payment Factor
10	8.94487	15	12.46146
10 1/4	9.11362	15 1/4	12.64321
10 1/2	9.28330	15 1/2	12.82534
10 3/4	9.45386	15 3/4	13.00785
11	9.62529	16	13.19070
11 1/4	9.79755	16 1/4	13.37388
11 1/2	9.97061	16 1/2	13.55737
11 3/4	10.14443	16 3/4	13.74114
12	10.31900	17	13.92520
12 1/4	10.49427	17 1/4	14.10950
12 1/2	10.67023	17 1/2	14.29405
12 3/4	10.84684	17 3/4	14.47882
13	11.02408	18	14.66380
13 1/4	11.20191	18 1/4	14.84897
13 1/2	11.38032	18 1/2	15.03432
13 3/4	11.55928	18 3/4	15.21984
14	11.73877	19	15.40550
14 1/4	11.91875	19 1/4	15.59131
14 1/2	12.09921	19 1/2	15.77724
14 3/4	12.28012	19 3/4	15.96329
		20	16.14944

*Interest being compounded semiannually.

APPENDIXES

APPENDIX A

Sources of Further Information

Contents

A. Condominiums
   1. National Real Estate Companies
   2. Provincial Home Builders' Associations
   3. Provincial New Home Warranty Programs
   4. Provincial Government Publication Departments
   5. Provincial Government Consumer Protection Departments
   6. Canada Mortgage and Housing Corporation
B. Condominium Associations
C. Condominium Publications
D. Timesharing Councils
E. Timesharing Exchange Companies
F. Timesharing Brokers
G. Co-operative Associations/Federations
H. Financing

A. CONDOMINIUMS

1. National Real Estate Companies

Most of the major national real estate companies can offer pamphlets, brochures, or newsletters relating to condominiums and real estate in general. Look in the Yellow Pages under "Real Estate."

- Block Bros. Realty
- Canada Trust Realtor
- Century 21
- Montreal Trust Realtor
- Realty World

- Re/Max
- Royal LePage

2. Provincial Home Builders' Associations

For publications or further information, contact your provincial or local home builders' association. Check in the Yellow Pages under "Associations." The following are the provincial associations.

Canadian Home Builders' Association of British Columbia
c/o 3700 Willingdon Avenue
Burnaby, British Columbia V5G 3H2 (604) 432-7112

Alberta Home Builders' Association
#205—10544—114th Street
Edmonton, Alberta T5H 3J7 (403) 424-5890

Saskatchewan Home Builders' Association
857 Arcola Avenue
Regina, Saskatchewan S4N 0S9 (306) 569-2424

Manitoba Home Builders' Association
Suite 239
1120 Grant Avenue
Winnipeg, Manitoba R3M 2A6 (204) 477-5110

Ontario Home Builders' Association
5218 Yonge Street
Willowdale, Ontario M2N 5P6 (416) 229-2111

Association provinciale des constructeurs d'habitations
   du Québec Inc.
5800, boul. Louis-H. Lafontaine
Ville d'Anjou, Québec H1M 1S7 (514) 353-9960

Nova Scotia Home Builders' Association
41 Pine Street
Dartmouth, Nova Scotia B2Y 2W6 (902) 466-5862

New Brunswick Home Builders' Association
P.O. Box 272, Station A
Fredericton, New Brunswick E3B 4Y9 (506) 459-7129

Construction Association of P.E.I.
P.O. Box 728, 92 1/2 Queen Street
Charlottetown, Prince Edward Island C1A 7L3   (902) 368-3303

Newfoundland & Labrador Home Builders'
  Association Ltd.
718 Water Street
St. John's, Newfoundland A1E 1C1   (709) 753-2000

3. Provincial New Home Warranty Programs

For new home warranty program information in your province or region,
contact the office below.

New Home Warranty Program of British Columbia &
  The Yukon
Suite 760
1441 Creekside Drive
Vancouver, British Columbia V6B 3R9   (604) 736-9231

New Home Warranty Program of Alberta
#201—208—57th Avenue S.W.
Calgary, Alberta T2H 2K8   (403) 253-3636

New Home Warranty Program of Saskatchewan Inc.
3012 Louise Street
Saskatoon, Saskatchewan S7J 3L8   (306) 373-7833

New Home Warranty Program of Manitoba Inc.
Grant Park Plaza
#220—1120 Grant Avenue
Winnipeg, Manitoba R3M 2A6   (204) 477-1877

Ontario New Home Warranty Program
600 Eglinton Avenue East
Toronto, Ontario M4P 1P3   (416) 488-6000

La garantie des maisons neuves de l'APCHQ
5800, boul. Louis-H. Lafontaine
Ville d'Anjou, Québec H1M 1S7   (514) 353-1120

Atlantic New Home Warranty Corporation
P.O. Box 411
Halifax, Nova Scotia V3J 2P8   (902) 425-7225

4. Provincial Government Publication Departments

To obtain copies of statutes and regulations relating to condominiums, co-operatives, and real estate, contact the provincial government office below. Enquire as to the current cost.

Queen's Printer
Province of British Columbia
Parliament Buildings
Victoria, British Columbia V8V 1X4   (604) 387-6690

Alberta Publication Services
Public Affairs Bureau
Province of Alberta
11510 Kingsway Avenue
Edmonton, Alberta T5G 2Y5   (403) 427-4387

Acts & Publications
Saskatchewan Property Management Corp.
1st Floor East
3475 Albert Street
Regina, Saskatchewan S4S 6X6   (306) 787-6894

Office of the Queen's Printer
Province of Manitoba
Statutory Publications
200 Vaughan Street
Winnipeg, Manitoba R3C 1T5   (204) 945-3103

Ontario Government Bookstore
Province of Ontario
5th Floor
880 Bay Street
Toronto, Ontario M7A 1N8   (416) 965-6015

Ministère des communications
Direction générale des publications gouvernementales
11e étage
1279, boul. Charest ouest
Québec, Québec G1N 4K7   (418) 643-9810

Queen's Printer
Province of New Brunswick
P.O. Box 6000
Fredericton, New Brunswick E3B 5H1   (506) 453-2520

Government Bookstore
Province of Nova Scotia
P.O. Box 637
Halifax, Nova Scotia V3J 2T3   (902) 424-7580

Queen's Printer
Province of Prince Edward Island
P.O. Box 2000
Charlottetown, Prince Edward Island C1A 7N8   (902) 368-5190

Queen's Printer
Province of Newfoundland
P.O. Box 4750
St. John's, Newfoundland A1C 5T7   (709) 576-3649

5. Provincial Government Consumer Protection Departments

Many provinces have free brochures relating to consumers' rights and
cautions when buying homes, condominiums, or co-operatives. Contact
your provincial department for further information.

Ministry of Labour & Consumer Services
Province of British Columbia
1019 Wharf Street
Parliament Buildings
Victoria, British Columbia V8V 1X4   (604) 387-3194

Consumer & Corporate Affairs
Province of Alberta
22nd Floor
P.O. Box 1616, 10025 Jasper Avenue
Edmonton, Alberta T5J 2N9   (403) 427-4095

Consumer & Commercial Affairs
Province of Saskatchewan
1871 Smith Street
Regina, Saskatchewan S4P 3V7   (306) 787-5550

Consumers' Bureau
Province of Manitoba
114 Garry Street
Winnipeg, Manitoba R3C 1G1   (204) 956-2040

Consumer Advisory Services Branch
Ministry of Consumer & Commercial Relations
Province of Ontario
8th Floor
555 Yonge Street
Toronto, Ontario M4A 2H6   (416) 963-0321

Office de la protection du consommateur
400, boul. Jean-Lesage, bur. 450
Québec, Québec G1K 8W4   (418) 643-1484

Consumer Affairs Branch
Province of New Brunswick
Consumer Affairs Division, Department of Justice
P.O. Box 6000
Fredericton, New Brunswick E3B 5H1   (506) 453-2659

Consumer Services Division
Department of Consumer Affairs
Province of Nova Scotia
P.O. Box 998, 5151 Terminal Road
Halifax, Nova Soctia B3J 2X3   (902) 424-4690

Consumer Services Division
Province of Prince Edward Island
P.O. Box 2000
Charlottetown, Prince Edward Island C1A 7N8   (902) 368-4580

Consumer Affairs Division
Department of Consumer Affairs & Communications
Province of Newfoundland
P.O. Box 4750, Elizabeth Towers
St. John's, Newfoundland A1C 5T7   (709) 576-2591

6. Canada Mortgage and Housing Corporation

For a free catalogue of publications relating to condominiums, co-operatives, and financing real estate in general, contact the CMHC office in
your region. There are provincial offices as well as local branch offices

of CMHC in many Canadian communities. Check in the Blue Pages of your telephone directory under "Government of Canada." Regional and local offices are located in the following areas:

British Columbia
- Vancouver   (604) 731-5733
- Victoria   (604) 388-3103
- Cranbrook   (604) 489-4111
- Kelowna   (604) 860-3613
- Kamloops   (604) 372-1711
- Prince George   (604) 563-9216

Alberta
- Calgary   (403) 292-6200
- Lethbridge   (403) 328-5581
- Edmonton   (403) 482-8700

Saskatchewan
- Regina   (306) 780-5880
- Saskatoon   (306) 975-4900

Manitoba
- Winnipeg   (204) 983-5600

Ontario
- Ottawa   (613) 728-6884
- Kingston   (613) 547-2457
- Peterborough   (705) 743-3584
- Toronto   (416) 781-2451
- Oshawa   (416) 571-3200
- Hamilton   (416) 523-2451
- Barrie   (705) 728-4811
- Kitchener   (519) 743-5264
- London   (519) 438-1731
- Windsor   (519) 256-8221
- Sudbury   (705) 675-2206
- North Bay   (705) 472-7750
- Sault Ste. Marie   (705) 759-1116
- Thunder Bay   (807) 343-2010

Quebec
- Sept-Îles   (418) 962-5136
- Rimouski   (418) 722-3388
- Chicoutimi   (418) 549-2381

- Quebec City   (418) 651-2310
- Trois-Rivières   (819) 379-6133
- Sherbrooke   (819) 565-4220
- Montreal   (514) 283-2222
- Laval   (514) 663-9300
- Longueuil   (514) 670-4600
- Hull   (819) 770-1550
- Val-d'Or   (819) 824-3649

New Brunswick
- Moncton   (506) 857-6116
- Fredericton   (506) 452-3050
- Saint John   (506) 648-4988

Nova Scotia
- Halifax   (902) 426-3530
- Sydney   (902) 564-7840

Prince Edward Island
- Charlottetown   (902) 566-7336

Newfoundland
- St. John's   (709) 772-4400

Yukon Territory
- Whitehorse   (403) 667-4236

Northwest Territories
- Yellowknife   (403) 873-2638

B. CONDOMINIUM ASSOCIATIONS

The Canadian Condominium Institute has a quarterly newsletter, publications, seminars relating to condominium hiring and management, and
an annual conference. Members are condominium owners and those involved in the condominium industry, including professionals, condominium corporations, and unit owners. There are chapters in various provinces.
Contact the Institute for further information:

Canadian Condominium Institute
Suite 200
2949 Bathurst Street
Toronto, Ontario M6B 3B2   (416) 789-7137

C. CONDOMINIUM PUBLICATIONS

There are many publications available relating to real estate. Check your local newsstand and public library for local and provincial publications. Some you may wish to consider which relate to condominiums include:

Condominium Magazine (11 issues per year)
Suite 200
172 John Street
Toronto, Ontario M5T 1X5   (416) 585-2552
(Topics of general interest relating to condominiums in Canada.)

The Condominium Buyer's Guide (annual)
(Published by *Condominium* magazine [see above]. Profiles Toronto and area condominiums for sale. Includes special feature articles of general interest relating to condominium purchase.)

DEL Condominium Life (quarterly)
4800 Dufferin Street
Downsview, Ontario M3H 5S9   (416) 661-3640
(Articles of general interest. Distributed in Toronto and Ottawa.)

Royal LePage Survey of Canadian House Prices (quarterly)
(Includes condominiums. Contact a local Royal LePage office [head office address below] for a free copy.)

Condominium Living Newsletter (quarterly)
Royal LePage
Marketing Department
39 Wynford Drive
Don Mills, Ontario M3C 3K5   (416) 445-9500
(Available through any Royal LePage office.)

The Homeowner Newsletter (six times per year)
(Published by Royal LePage. For a free subscription, contact the above address.)

D. TIMESHARING COUNCILS

Timesharing councils comprise companies that are involved in recreational resorts and in residential real estate development relating to timeshares. Contact the following organizations for further information:

Resort Timesharing Council of Canada
48 Hayden Street
Toronto, Ontario M4Y 1V8   (416) 960-4930
(Available are: brochure on the concept of timesharing; *Directory of Resorts*.)

National Timesharing Council of the American Land Development
   Association
Suite 510—1220 "L" Street N.W.
Washington, D.C., U.S.A. 20005   (202) 371-6700
(Available are: *Resort and Urban Timesharing: A Consumer's Guide;
Directory of Resorts;* bibliography.)

E.   TIMESHARING EXCHANGE COMPANIES

Resorts Condominium International
3502 Woodview Trace
Indianapolis, Indiana, U.S.A. 462268   (317) 876-8899
(Available are: information pamphlet; directory of members from U.S.,
Canada, internationally.)

Interval International
6262 Sunset Drive
Penthouse 1
Miami, Florida, U.S.A. 33143   (305) 666-1861
(Available are: information pamphlet; directory of members from U.S.,
Canada, internationally.)

Exchange Network
P.O. Box 752
Ocean Springs, Mississippi, U.S.A. 39564   (601) 497-4666
(Available are: information pamphlet; directory of members from U.S.,
Canada, internationally.)

F.   TIMESHARING BROKERS

There are other timesharing brokers as well as this. Contact the National
Timesharing Council of the American Land Development Association for
a current list.

Timeshare Re-Sale International Inc.
17 East Weaver Avenue
Harrisonberg, Virginia, U.S.A. 22801   (703) 434-7787
(Available are: information pamphlet; directory of timeshares for sale in
U.S., Canada, internationally.)

G. CO-OPERATIVE ASSOCIATIONS/FEDERATIONS

Co-operative Housing Foundation of Canada
Suite 202
275 Bank Street
Ottawa, Ontario K2P 2L6   (613) 238-4644
(Contact CHF for a list of publications and a directory of housing cooperatives.)

The various provincial co-op federations are:

Co-operative Housing Federation of British Columbia
4676 Main Street
Vancouver, B.C. V5V 3R7   (604) 879-5111

Vancouver Island Co-operative Housing Association
#102—927 Old Esquimalt Road
Victoria, British Columbia V9A 4X4   (604) 384-9444

Northern Alberta Co-operative Housing Association
c/o 10551—123rd Street
Edmonton, Alberta T5N 1N9   (403) 482-5467

Southern Alberta Co-operative Housing Association
c/o #303—1725—10th Avenue S.W.
Calgary, Alberta T3C 0K1   (403) 228-0431

Co-operative Housing Association of Saskatchewan
P.O. Box 5005
Saskatoon, Saskatchewan S7K 4ES   (306) 242-3818

Housing Co-op Council of Manitoba
32 Shelmerdine Drive
Winnipeg, Manitoba R3R 2Y2   (204) 888-7838

Co-operative Housing Federation of Toronto
Suite 401
151 John Street
Toronto, Ontario M5V 2T2   (416) 598-1641

Co-operative Housing Association of Hamilton
Suite 207
845 Upper James
Hamilton, Ontario L9A 3C3   (416) 575-7577

Peel-Halton Inter Co-op Council
P.O. Box 1364, Station B
Mississauga, Ontario L4Y 4B6   (416) 828-4530

Ottawa Federation of Housing Co-ops
5th Floor
200 Isabella Street
Ottawa, Ontario K1S 1V7   (613) 238-5141

Regroupement des co-operatives d'habitation
   de l'Outaouaise
12, rue Babot
Hull, Québec J8X 3E1   (819) 770-2330

Fédération des co-operatives d'habitation Monterégiennes
885, ave. Ste-Hélène
Longueuil, Québec J4K 3R7   (514) 674-4678

Fédération des co-operatives d'habitation populaire
   des cantons de l'est
126, rue Brooks
Sherbrooke, Québec J1H 4X8   (819) 565-1813

Fédération des co-operatives d'habitation de l'Île
   de Montréal
744, rue Atwater
Montréal, Québec H4C 2B9   (514) 931-5740

Regroupement des co-operatives d'habitation du Bas
   du Fleuve
A/S 30, Eveche est, bureau 401
Rimouski, Québec G5L 1X6   (418) 722-8535

Fédération régionale des co-operatives d'habitation
   du Québec
1080, rue de la Chevrotière
Québec, Québec G1R 3J4   (418) 648-1354

Comité de liaison co-ops GRT
A/S 411, rue Rouleau, app. 1
Rimouski, Québec E5L 5W6   (418) 725-8618

Co-operative Housing Federation of Nova Scotia
6074 Lady Hammond Road
Halifax, Nova Scotia V3K 2R7   (902) 453-0680

Co-operative Housing Association of Newfoundland
   and Labrador
c/o 58 Warberry Street
St. John's, Newfoundland A1C 1P1   (709) 753-9860

H. FINANCING

Most bankers, trust companies, and credit unions have free publications
relating to mortgages and other financing information. Contact your local
branches of the major chartered banks for current publications.

Canadian Bankers' Association
Suite 600
The Exchange Tower
2 First Canadian Place
Toronto, Ontario M5X 1E1   (416) 362-6092
(Several free publications are available on request, including *Mortgage
Wise* and *Credit Wise.*)

APPENDIX B

Suggested Reading

Note: Asterisks (*) denote Canadian content.

A. Condominiums and Co-operatives

Aronson, Jake. *289 Most Asked Questions on Condominiums Answered.* Dayton, Ohio: Landfall Press, 1984.

Blagden, Nellie and Edith P. Marshall. *The Complete Condo and Co-op Information Book.* New York: Holt Mifflin, 1983.

Brooks, Patricia and Lester Brooks. *How to Buy a Condominium.* New York: Stein & Day Publishers, 1975.

*Burns, Audrey L. and Bradley N. McLellan. *Condominiums: The Law and Administration in Ontario.* Toronto: The Carswell Company Limited, 1981.

Bush, Vanessa A. *Condominiums and Cooperatives.* Chicago: Contemporary Books, 1986.

Cassidy, Bruce. *The Complete Condominium Guide.* New York: Dodd, Mead and Company, 1979.

Clurman, David. *The Business Condominium.* New York: John Wiley & Sons, 1973.

Clurman, David and Edna L. Hebard. *Condominiums and Cooperatives.* New York: John Wiley & Sons, 1970.

The Condominium Community: A Guide for Owners, Boards, and Managers. Chicago: Institute of Real Estate Management, 1978.

*Fanaken, Gerry. *Improving the Condominium Concept: Ideas for Change.* Vancouver: Vancouver Condominium Services Ltd., 1987.

*———. *Understanding the Condominium Concept: A Handbook for B.C.* Vancouver: Vancouver Condominium Services Ltd., 1987.

Goldstick, David T. and Carolyn Janik. *The Complete Guide to Co-ops and Condominiums.* New York: New American Library, 1983.

Gray, Genevieve. *Condominiums: How to Buy, Sell and Live in Them.* New York: Funk & Wagnalls, 1975.

*Hamilton, Stan W. *Condominiums: A Decade of Experience.* Vancouver: British Columbia Real Estate Association, 1978.

Karr, James N. *The Condominium Buyer's Guide.* New York: Frederick Fell Publishers, 1973.

Kaufman, Phyllis C. and Arnold Corrigan. *Understanding Condominiums and Co-ops.* Stamford, Connecticut: Long Meadow Press, 1985.

Kennedy, David W. *The Condominium and Cooperative Apartment Buyer's and Seller's Guide.* New York: John Wiley & Sons, 1983.

178

Kiev, Phyllis. *The Woman's Guide to Buying Houses, Co-ops & Condominiums.* New York: Ballantine, 1981.

Lee, Steven J. *Buyer's Handbook for Cooperatives & Condominiums.* New York: Van Nostrand Reinhold, 1983.

*Marks, Anthony. *Understanding Condominiums and Cooperatives: A Comprehensive Practical Handbook.* Vancouver: Lansdowne Row Co., 1980.

Mettler, Helen. *The Co-op and Condo Owner's Handbook.* New York: HRM Communications Inc., 1983.

*Pavlich, Dennis J. *Condominium Law in British Columbia.* Toronto: Butterworths, 1983.

*————. *The Strata Titles Act.* Toronto: Butterworths, 1978.

*Rosenberg, Alvin B. *Condominium in Canada.* Toronto: Canada Law Book Limited, 1969.

Tymon, Dorothy. *The Condominium: A Guide for the Alert Buyer.* New York: Avon Books, 1978.

B. Timeshares

Block, Stuart M. and William B. Ingersoll, eds. *Timesharing.* Washington: Urban Land Institute, 1977.

Burlingame, Carl H., ed. *The Buyer's Guide to Resort Timesharing.* Los Altos, California: The CHB Company, Inc., 1980.

*Coltman, Michael M. *Resort Condos and Timesharing.* Vancouver: International Self-Counsel Press Ltd., 1981.

*Marks, Anthony. *Real Estate Time-Sharing: With 64 Original Applications.* Toronto: CCH Canadian Limited, 1986.

Rose, Donald K. *The Vacation-Condo Game.* Aurora, Colorado: The National Writers' Press, 1984.

*Spencer, Phyllis. *Vacation Timesharing.* Toronto: Personal Library Publishers, 1982.

Trowbridge, Keith W. *Resort Timesharing.* New York: Simon & Schuster, 1981.

C. Real Estate

(These works include chapters on condos and co-ops.)

*Rose, Stanley M. *Real Estate Buying/Selling Guide for Ontario.* Vancouver: International Self-Counsel Press Ltd., 1985.

*Silverstein, Alan. *Home Buying Strategies for Newly Built Homes.* Toronto: Stoddard Publishing, 1987.

*————. *Home Buying Strategies for Resale Homes.* Toronto: Stoddard Publishing, 1986.

*Steacy, Richard. *Canadian Real Estate.* Toronto: Stoddard Publishing, 1986.

*Stewart, George C. *Real Estate Buying/Selling Guide for Alberta.* Vancouver: International Self-Counsel Press Ltd., 1985.

*Syberg-Olsen, E. *Real Estate Buying/Selling Guide for B.C.* Vancouver: International Self-Counsel Press Ltd., 1986.

Thomsett, Michael C. *How to Buy a Home, Condo or Co-Op.* New York: Consumers' Union of U.S. Inc., 1987.

*Weiss, Gary. *The Small Investor's Guide to Making Money in Canadian Real Estate.* Toronto: Stoddard Publishing, 1987.

*Zimmer, Henry. *How to Profit from the Next Real Estate Boom.* Edmonton: Hurtig Publishers, 1984.

D. Mortgages

*Cohen, Kenneth J. *Canadian Home Mortgage Manual.* Toronto: Checkerbooks, 1982.

*Costello, Brian. *Making Money from Your Mortgage.* Toronto: Random House, 1987.

*Goldenberg, David M. *Mortgages and Foreclosure.* Vancouver: International Self-Counsel Press Ltd., 1983.

*Silverstein, Alan. *Hidden Profits in Your Mortgage.* Toronto: Stoddard Publishing, 1985.

*Steacy, Richard. *A Practical Canadian Mortgage Guide.* Toronto: Stoddard Publishing, 1979.

APPENDIX C
Glossary

Administrators In Quebec, those persons the co-ownership has appointed to act as administrators of the immoveables. Equivalent to *board of directors* or *condominium council*. The administrators are responsible to the co-proprietors and are entrusted with the conservation of the immoveables and the maintenance and administration of the common portions.

Agreement of purchase and sale A written agreement between the developer and a condominium or timesharer for purchase of a condominium or timeshare unit; or, in the case of a resale, a written agreement between the condominium or timesharer owner of a unit and a purchaser. Used loosely in connection with all forms of timesharing. Also referred to as *purchase and sale agreement*.

Amenities Generally, those parts of the common property and its facilities that are intended to beautify the premises, and which are for the enjoyment of occupants rather than for utility.

Amortization period The actual number of years it will take to repay a mortgage loan in full. This can be well in excess of the loan's term. For example, mortgages often have 5-year terms but 25-year amortization periods.

Appraised value An estimate of the value of the property offered as security for a mortgage loan. This appraisal is done for mortgage lending purposes and may not reflect the market value of the property.

Assessment fee Also referred to as *maintenance fee*. A monthly fee which condominium lot owners must pay, usually including management fees, costs of common-property upkeep, heating costs, garbage removal costs, the owner's contribution to the contingency reserve fund, and so on. In the case of timeshares, the fee is normally levied annually.

Assumption agreement A legal document signed by a home buyer which requires the buyer to assume responsibility for the obligations of a mortgage made by a former owner.

Balance sheet A financial statement that indicates the financial status of an association, condominium, corporation, or timeshare project at a specific point in time by listing its assets, liabilities, and members' equity.

Blended payments Equal payments consisting of both a principal and an interest component, paid each month during the term of the mortgage. The principal portion increases each month, while the interest portion decreases; but the total monthly payment does not change.

Board of directors The directors of the condominium corporation formed under the statute. Sometimes called just "the Board." In most provinces non–unit owners may be elected to the board. In Quebec the responsibilities of the "administrators" are generally the same as those for the board of directors in other provinces. Directors may have personal liability exposure.

Budget An annual estimate of the project's expenses and revenues needed to balance those expenses. There are *operating* budgets and *capital* budgets. (See also *Capital budget.*)

Buildings The buildings included in a property, usually referring to the parts which are divided into the units and the common elements.

By-laws One of the documents used in the conferring of condominium status. By-laws are included in the condominium statute in British Columbia, Alberta, and Saskatchewan. In other provinces, by-laws have to be created, but the words of the by-laws are not contained in the statute. By-laws deal with the operational aspects of the condominium corporation and the duties and responsibilities of the board of directors. (See also *Statutory by-laws.*)

Canada Mortgage and Housing Corporation (CMHC) The federal Crown corporation which administers the National Housing Act. CMHC services include providing housing information and assistance, financing, and insuring home purchase loans for lenders.

Capital budget An estimate of costs to cover replacements and improvements, and the corresponding revenues needed to balance them, usually for a 12-month period. Different from an *operating budget* (which see).

Charge A document registered against a property, stating that someone has or believes he or she has a claim on the property.

Closing The actual completion of the transaction acknowledging satisfaction of all legal and financial obligations between buyer and seller, and acknowledging the deed or transfer of title and disbursement of funds to appropriate parties.

Closing costs The expenses over and above the purchase price of buying and selling real estate.

Closing date The date on which the sale of a property becomes final and the new owner takes possession.

Club membership timeshare One of the non–fee simple right-to-use forms of timesharing. It consists of a simple contract for use of a particular kind of unit, without specifying the unit, for a given number of years in a non-profit association. Club memberships are usually non-transferable; or if this is not the case, the club's approval is required beforehand. The contract may provide for a right of first refusal in favour of the club. Usually a club membership cannot be sold for more than the original price.

Collateral mortgage A loan backed up by a promissory note and the security of a mortgage on a property. The money borrowed may be used for the purchase of the property itself or for another purpose, such as home renovations or a vacation.

Common elements   Those parts of the property that are owned in common by the unit owners (e.g., halls, elevators, parking area, swimming pool, etc.). In British Columbia, Alberta, and Saskatchewan they are referred to as *common property*, and in Quebec, as *common portions*. Under all Canadian statutes, whatever the term used, it means all of the property except the units. (See also *Limited common elements*.)

Common expenses   Expenses incurred by the condominium corporation in carrying out the duties and responsibilities as specified in the project documents—e.g., in the declaration.

Common funds   Funds (such as a contingency/reserve fund) held by the corporation or administrators of the co-ownership of the immoveables, but belonging to the unit owners.

Common interest   The proportional interest in the common elements belonging to a unit owner. (See also *Unit proportion*.)

Condominium   A housing unit to which the owner has title and which the owner also owns a share in the common elements of (such as elevators, hallways, swimming pool, land, etc.).

Condominium council   The governing body of the condominium corporation, elected at the annual general meeting of the corporation. Similar to a *board of directors* (which see).

Condominium legislation   The legislation enacted by the provinces and territories to permit both individual and shared ownership of portions of multi-unit developments. Describes what a condominium is, how one is created, and how it must be administered. Provinces may from time to time make significant changes to their legislation. For reliable guidance the reader should always refer to the most recent provincial legislation.

Condominium management   The firm or individual responsible for managing and maintaining the physical and financial administration aspects of a condominium. Hired by the board of directors.

Condominium plan   In Alberta and Saskatchewan, the plan which is registered and which in essence describes the total project and each of the units in it. (See also *Declaration* and *Description*.)

Contingency fund   (See *Reserve fund*.)

Conventional mortgage   A mortgage loan which does not exceed 75% of the appraised value or of the purchase price of the property, whichever is the lesser. Mortgages that exceed this limit must be insured by mortgage insurance, such as that provided by CMHC and MICC.

Conversion   The changing of a structure from some other use such as a rental apartment to a condominium apartment.

Conveyancing   The transfer of property, or title to property, from one party to another.

Co-operative   A form of ownership in which the individual "owner" has a share in the co-operative, which body actually owns the property. The "owner" has the right to live in a housing unit by means of a lease, but does not own the actual unit.

Co-proprietor   In Quebec, a unit owner. The actual form of ownership is called *co-ownership*.

Corporation   The condominium association of unit owners incorporated under some Condominium Acts automatically at the time of registration of the project. It is called *strata corporation* in British Columbia. Under each of the statutes it will differ from an ordinary corporation in many respects. The corporation, unlike a private business corporation, does not enjoy limited liability, and any judgement against the corporation for the payment of money is also a judgement against each owner. The objects of the corporation are to manage the property and any assets of the corporation, and its duties include effecting compliance by the owners with the requirements of the Act, the declaration, the by-laws, and the rules.

Declaration   The document used in Ontario, Manitoba, Nova Scotia, New Brunswick, Newfoundland, the Yukon Territory, and the Northwest Territories that complies with the formal requirements of the Condominium Act and which, upon registration, submits the project to the provisions of the Act and creates the condominium. It is called a *condominium plan* in Alberta and Saskatchewan and a *strata plan* in British Columbia. In Quebec it is known as the *declaration of co-ownership*.

Deed   This document conveys the title of the property to the purchaser. Different terminology may be used in different provincial jurisdictions.

Description   In Ontario, Nova Scotia, Newfoundland, and New Brunswick, the document which is registered simultaneously with the declaration and which defines the total project and describes each unit. Sets out those parts of the condominium development that are to be privately owned, and those areas that are to be owned in common by the owners.

Destruction   A legal concept. When a condominium project is seriously damaged, the owners must decide whether or not to rebuild it. If they decide the latter, the project undergoes destruction, is *destroyed*, a legal process which divides the condominium corporation's assets among its owners. In certain circumstances condominium owners can also "destroy" a corporation even if it has not been damaged.

Development   The building or buildings and the land upon which they are situated. Sometimes used interchangeably with *project* (which see).

Disclosure statement   A series of documents prepared by the developer and issued to proposed unit purchasers describing the property and containing a budget statement for a set period immediately following the registration of the condominium. Until the purchaser receives a copy of the current disclosure statement, the agreement of purchase and sale can be voided by the purchaser, under Ontario legislation.

Down payment An initial amount of money (in the form of cash) put forward by the purchaser. Usually it represents the difference between the purchase price and the amount of the mortgage loan.

Encumbrance (See *Charge.*)

Equity The difference between the price for which a property could be sold and the total debts registered against it.

Escrow The holding of a deed or contract by a third party until fulfillment of certain stipulated conditions between the contracting parties.

Estate The title or interest one has in property such as real estate and personal property that can, if desired, be passed on to survivors at the time of one's death.

Estoppel certificate A written statement requested by the prospective purchaser of a resale unit. The estoppel outlines whether or not all maintenance fees and other payments to be made by the current unit owner are up to date. In addition, it outlines other important financial or legal considerations.

Exclusive portion In Quebec, the parts of the immoveables owned by and reserved for the private use of the individual proprietor. (See *Unit.*)

Fee simple A manner of owning land: in one's own name and free of any conditions, limitations, or restrictions.

Financial statements Documents which show the financial status of the condominium corporation, cooperative, or timeshare project at a given point in time. Generally includes income and expense statement and balance sheet.

Fiscal year The 12-month period in which financial affairs are calculated.

Floating-rate mortgage Another term for *variable-rate mortgage.*

Foreclosure A legal procedure whereby the lender obtains ownership of the property following default by the borrower.

Fraction In Quebec, an exclusive portion and a share of the common portions, under the civil code. Each co-proprietor has an undivided right of ownership in the common portions; his share in the common portions is equal to the value of the exclusive portion of his fraction in relation to the aggregate of the values of the exclusive portions.

High-ratio mortgage A conventional mortgage loan which exceeds 75% of the appraised value or purchase price of the property. Such a mortgage must be insured.

Immoveables   In Quebec, in reference to condominiums, all the land and buildings comprised in the condominium project.

Lien   A claim for the payment of money against a unit or a condominium corporation.

Limited common elements   Those common elements whose use is restricted to one or more unit owners or, conversely, those which are not available for use by all unit owners. These areas are often referred to as *exclusive-use areas*.

Maintenance fees   Fees for the upkeep of a project based on a unit owner's percentage share of operating and administrative costs of the condominium corporation. (See *Assessment fee.*)

Management agreement   A contract between representatives of the condominium or timeshare project and a management company to provide management services for the project's day-to-day operation and also to provide overall administrative services.

Mortgagee   The lender.

Mortgage Insurance Company of Canada (MICC)   A private company with offices across Canada providing mortgage insurance for lenders.

Mortgagor   The borrower.

National Housing Act (NHA) Loan   A mortgage loan which is insured by CMHC to certain maximums.

Offer to purchase   The document which sets forth all the terms and conditions under which a purchaser offers to purchase his unit. This offer, when accepted by the seller, becomes a binding agreement of purchase and sale.

Operating budget   An estimate of costs to operate the project and corresponding revenues needed to balance them, usually for a 12-month period. Different from a *capital budget* (which see).

Phantom mortgage   A technique developers of new condo units may use to compensate for the legal requirement to pay interest on the purchaser's deposit toward the purchase price. Comes into operation once a unit purchaser enters into interim occupancy pending the registration of the condominium by the developer. Under the condominium legislation of some provinces, the developer can charge an "occupation rent," which consists of common expenses for the unit, an estimate of municipal taxes for the unit, and interest on any mortgage the purchaser is required to assume or provide under the terms of the agreement of purchase and sale. A vendor (developer) take-back mortgage, payable on demand, is inserted in the agreement. The demand is normally made at the time of closing or within seven days; the mortgage is therefore "phantom." By inserting this provision, the developer obtains the right to charge interest on the balance of the purchase price, which could be more than the amount the developer has to pay the purchaser in interest on the deposit money. Since the legal enforceability of a given phantom mortgage might be questionable, legal advice should be obtained.

PI   Principal and interest due on a mortgage.

PIT   Principal, interest, and taxes due on a mortgage.

Principal   The amount you actually borrowed, or the portion of it still owing on the original loan.

Project   The entire parcel to be divided into units and common elements.

Project documents   The documents required to create a condominium, including, where such are applicable in the provincial jurisdiction, the declaration, the plan, the description, and the by-laws.

Prospectus   A written presentation prepared by the developer that outlines material facts about the offering to induce offers from prospective purchasers.

Purchase and sale agreement   (See *Agreement of purchase and sale.*)

Recision   That period of time following the sale during which the buyer can change his mind, cancel the purchase agreement, and get a refund of funds paid on deposit. It varies from province to province from 3 to 30 days.

Reserve fund   A fund set up to cover major repair and replacement costs or other unforeseen expenditures. In many provinces a percentage of all monthly maintenance fees must be put toward the reserve fund, and it is non-refundable. A healthy fund makes special assessments unnecessary.

Resource group   The entity which organizes people who are interested in joining new housing co-operatives. Generally involved in developing the co-op as well.

Rules and regulations   Rules which the board adopts respecting the use of the common elements and units to promote the safety and security of owners and property.

Schedule of interests upon destruction   A schedule showing the proportionate amounts of the land and assets of a condominium corporation due to the individual strata lot owners upon the destruction of the corporation. (See *Destruction.*)

Special assessment   An assessment above and beyond the monthly assessment, which the condominium council (for larger expenditures, generally 75% of the strata corporation members) may decide to levy for a special purpose, e.g., building a sauna or swimming pool. For unexpected or unbudgeted expenses.

Special resolution A resolution generally requiring approval of 75% of the condominium unit owners. Required for granting easements, acquiring or disposing of common property, passing by-laws, etc.

Statutory by-laws By-laws of the corporation set out as schedules to the Condominium Acts of British Columbia, Alberta, and Saskatchewan. Automatically in force when the Act is invoked until repealed or amended by a new provincial statute.

Strata corporation In British Columbia, equivalent to the term *corporation*.

Strata lot Term used in British Columbia to describe property subject to individual ownership. Similar to *unit* (which see).

Strata plan (See *Declaration* and *Description.*)

Title Generally, the evidence of right which a person has to the possession of property.

Title insurance A type of insurance that guarantees the status of a property's title against all defects. Term commonly used in the United States.

Undivided interest An individual condominium or timeshare owner's partial interest in the project's common property that is not defined by boundaries but is an abstraction.

Unit In all provinces except British Columbia and Quebec, each part of the project subject to individual ownership. In Ontario this comprises not only the space enclosed by the unit boundaries, but all material parts of the land within the space at the time the declaration and description are registered. In British Columbia, called *strata lot*, and in Quebec, *exclusive portion*.

Unit entitlement The share of a condominium owner in the common property, common facilities, and other assets of the strata corporation.

Unit factor In Alberta and Saskatchewan, the share ownership in the common elements separate from the unit. The same factor also relates to voting rights and contribution towards common expenses. (See *Unit proportion.*)

Unit proportion Generally, the proportion of the total common expenses that a condominium unit holder is responsible for.

Vendor A person selling a piece of property.

Vendor take-back A procedure wherein the seller (vendor) of a property provides some or all of the mortgage financing in order to sell the property. Also referred to as *vendor financing*.

INDEX

About the Author

Douglas A. Gray is one of Canada's foremost experts on real estate. As a lawyer dealing in real estate and commercial law, he frequently acts for buyers, sellers, lenders, and borrowers on residential and commercial real estate and mortgage matters. He gives seminars and presentations throughout Canada to professional realtor associations, real estate boards and companies, real estate investment clubs, and the general public.

Mr. Gray is regularly interviewed by the media as an authority on real estate and small business issues. He is the author of several bestselling business books, including *The Complete Canadian Small Business Guide* (McGraw-Hill Ryerson).

Mr. Gray is the founder and president of the Canadian Enterprise Institute and Enterprise Development International Inc.

Douglas A. Gray lives in Vancouver, British Columbia.

Reader Input and Brochure

If you have thoughts or suggestions that you believe would be helpful for future editions of this book, are interested in having a seminar or presentation given to your group or association, or would like to receive a brochure of other real estate educational products and material, please write to the author:

> Douglas A. Gray
> c/o Canadian Enterprise Institute
> Suite 310—1070 West Broadway
> Vancouver, B.C.
> V6H 1E7